The CAMPFIRE CAST IRON Cookbook

The Campfire Cast Iron Cookbook

13-Digit ISBN: 978-1-64643-130-4
10-Digit ISBN: 1-64643-130-8

This book may be ordered by mail from the publisher. Please include $5.99 for
postage and handling. Please support your local bookseller first!

Books published by Cider Mill Press Book Publishers are available at special
discounts for bulk purchases in the United States by corporations, institutions, and
other organizations. For more information, please contact the publisher.

Cider Mill Press Book Publishers
"Where good books are ready for press"
PO Box 454
12 Spring Street
Kennebunkport, Maine 04046

Visit us online!
cidermillpress.com

Typography: Adobe Jenson Pro, Livermore Script ATF Rough, Metallophile

Image Credits: Photos on pages 28, 89, 141, and 142 courtesy of Cider Mill Press.
All other images used under official license from Shutterstock.com.

Front cover image: Chicken with Herbs, see page 91.
Back cover images: Hungarian Goulash, see page 113; Pesto Chicken with Charred
Tomatoes, see page 106; Blueberry Pie, see page 189.

Printed in China
1 2 3 4 5 6 7 8 9 0
First Edition

The
CAMPFIRE CAST IRON
Cookbook

The Ultimate Cookbook of Hearty and Delicious Cast Iron Recipes

CIDER MILL PRESS

BOOK PUBLISHERS

KENNEBUNKPORT, MAINE

CONTENTS

INTRODUCTION

Outdoor cooking is best with cast iron and an open fire. Using cast-iron cookware outdoors is rustic and satisfying. It's also a bit of an art, and not quite as simple as just having the right tools. There are several things you need to factor in before tackling it for the first time. Once you've mastered the basics, though, you'll be off and running and won't ever need to look back.

There are a few methods you can use for cooking with cast iron over a campfire. The first, and arguably the most popular, is the cast-iron skillet. To use a skillet over a campfire, you can place it on a grate while wearing a heavy mitt. No matter what you're cooking, you'll need a small amount of fat in a hot pan, the product—a sausage, a freshly caught and cleaned fish, or even some nice vegetables—seasoning, and heat. This also works for Dutch ovens.

The suspended Dutch oven is the ideal method for making campfire baked beans, chili, stews, and soups. You will need at least one-third of the vessel to have liquid (stock, broth, wine, water, etc.), then you're free to fill the rest with your selections of vegetables, protein, beans, hearty grains, and seasonings. As your meal cooks, make sure to stir periodically.

Another popular option is the coal-top Dutch oven. Many Dutch ovens have a distinct lip on the lid. This feature was designed for you to place hot coals on top—using very long, strong tongs. This creates more of an oven atmosphere within the pot. For this method, place the oven on a grate or heat plate. Fill the Dutch oven with your food and cover the lid with coals. While the exact number of coals that will benefit a specific recipe will vary and can only be determined through experience, a good rule of thumb to determine how many coals you'll need to maintain heat is to multiply the size of your Dutch oven by two, then put one-third of the coals below and two-thirds on top. For a 12-inch Dutch oven, you will want around eight coals underneath and 16 on top, evenly spaced. You will also need to rotate the pot occasionally, since the heat of your fire will be uneven.

Before you start cooking outdoors, however, the absolute first thing to do is make sure the surroundings are perfectly safe. If you'll be cooking in a public area like a park or campground, you need to seek out and check all posted signs and make sure fires are allowed, and, if so, that it hasn't been designated a "high fire risk" day. If your area doesn't issue fire warnings, use your best judgment. Additionally, take a look and see if there are any major hazards. There should be no dry material within 10 feet of where you'll be building the fire. The area around your firepit or campfire should be cleared of any debris or otherwise flammable materials.

If you're making your own pit, dig your hole 1 foot deep and 2 to 3 feet across and encircle the pit with rocks. If you're using an existing pit or grill, make sure there is no debris or trash that needs to be removed. Other users may not have been as conscientious or courteous as you.

The essentials you need to build a fire are as follows: charcoal or firewood; a shovel; a charcoal chimney starter; a long lighter or matches; heavy gloves; a bucket of water. Please note that while using lighter fluid makes starting a fire easier, it doesn't make it better; the preferred method is the tried-and true combination of fire and wood. Lighter fluid has fumes and is not ideal to travel with.

You have a few different options for building your fire. If you are using wood to build a fire, collect a combination of dry and cured small twigs—or tinder—dry leaves, medium branches, and larger logs. Make sure your wood is cut or broken to fit in the pit. Put the twigs and leaves in the center of your firepit. Now you want to build a cone sculpture. It should be about 2 feet tall. Using a long match or stick lighter, carefully ignite the leaves at the bottom of the cone from a few angles. As the fire builds and burns, carefully add larger pieces of wood to keep it going. Never leave your fire unattended. A note if using firewood: only use firewood that you have purchased from a reputable source, or collect wood from the immediate area where you will be cooking. Always make sure you are burning nontoxic woods (and never poison oak), and remember that using non-native wood can have serious ecological impact through the inadvertent relocation of insects and diseases.

If using charcoal, loosely wad up a few pieces of paper and place a charcoal chimney starter on top, in the center of your firepit. Fill the chimney almost to the top with charcoal. Using a long match or stick lighter, light the paper on fire from the bottom. The coals will be red-hot and covered with a light layer of white ash in about 15 minutes. When they're ready, pour the coals into the center of your pit or grill. Place the empty chimney someplace safe to cool.

Once your fire is lit and has had a while to burn down (you never want to cook over flames that are shooting up) you're ready to cook. Keep in mind that cooking over a fire takes longer than cooking over a stove and requires more attention. Now you have to decide: Do you want to cook on a grate or use a tripod? A grate is best if you will be using a skillet or Dutch oven. A tripod is the only choice if you're using a round bottomed cauldron or a Dutch oven with a hanging loop handle (that part is essential). You also have the option of cooking directly on the fire, which is best done with three-legged cauldrons or a skillet. Lastly, you can bury a Dutch oven into the embers directly.

To set up a grate for cooking, make sure it is as level as possible, and that it will not fall over. It should be sturdy enough to hold all of the cookware you plan on placing on it. Set the grate over the fire using gloved hands and tongs.

Tripods have three legs and a sturdy chain that hangs from the center. Set it up prior to building your fire. Make sure it is very stable and that it can handle the weight of a full Dutch oven. You can purchase tripods at well-equipped camping stores; alternately, there are kits available online.

The beauty of cast iron is the heat, and that's what these recipes reflect. The heat of the fire can't be regulated, but you can determine where the hotter and cooler spots are. The edges of the fire will of course be cooler, so place most of your pots and pans to the side. With this method, you will need to keep an eye on everything. Also, the higher up your pot or pan is, the further it is from the heat and the less chance there will be burning. The best meals cooked over a campfire are the ones that have only a few ingredients, all of which come to life when kissed by fire. To make the most of your experience, try to do a lot of the prep work for your meal before you head out. Have all of the ingredients, tools, and equipment you will need ready to go. Aluminum foil can be a lifesaver, too. Never leave a roll behind when you're heading into the great outdoors.

One of the best parts about cooking with cast iron is the easy cleanup, which is especially attractive at a campsite. When you have removed all of the food from your cast-iron cookware, add a bit of water. When the water has cooled slightly, use a good stiff brush or scrubbing pad to clean it. Rinse and dry as thoroughly as possible. Your cast iron will rust out in nature just as easily as at home. What you never want to do when you are outdoors is use salt to clean your pans. It's still effective, but it's not easy to dispose of large amounts. Throwing salt on the ground or in a freshwater lake or river can kill plants and animals.

Another extremely important part of cleanup is caring for your firepit. When you're done with your firepit, you need to make sure there's no danger of it reigniting and check that you haven't littered or polluted the area. Make sure you check out the USDA Forest Service guidelines for extinguishing a campfire.

Cooking outdoors doesn't mean you have to limit yourself. This is a book in which every recipe has been written for cast-iron cookware over a campfire. Take some time with this book and you'll see how incredibly varied the recipes are. From satisfying breakfasts to complementary sides, succulent meats, delectable vegetables, and rich desserts, you'll soon see that your campsite is completed by cast iron.

BREAKFAST

Sometimes breakfast at a campsite is as simple as grabbing a piece of fruit and running off to explore the outdoors. But other times we want, or really need, to sidle up to the fire and take a few minutes to make something that is worth lingering over. No matter what you pick to get your day started off on the right foot, you can proceed knowing that, thanks to your

Rosemary & Black Pepper Scones

YIELD: 4 TO 6 SERVINGS • ACTIVE TIME: 30 MINUTES • TOTAL TIME: 50 MINUTES

While these are a bit savory for an early breakfast, they are a hit for brunch, when they can very nicely complement a simple omelette.

INGREDIENTS

3 CUPS ALL-PURPOSE FLOUR, PLUS MORE FOR DUSTING

2½ TEASPOONS BAKING POWDER

½ TEASPOON BAKING SODA

1 TEASPOON SALT

1½ STICKS OF UNSALTED BUTTER, CHILLED, AND CUT INTO PIECES

1 TABLESPOON DRIED ROSEMARY

1 TABLESPOON FRESHLY GROUND BLACK PEPPER

1 CUP WHOLE MILK OR HALF-AND-HALF

DIRECTIONS

1 Position a grate over the fire using gloved hands and tongs. Make sure the grate is as secure and level as possible.

2 In a large bowl, whisk together the flour, baking powder, baking soda, and salt. Add the butter pieces and mix with a fork so that the dough is somewhat crumbly.

3 Stir in the rosemary, black pepper, and milk or half-and-half, being careful not to overmix.

4 With flour on your hands, transfer the dough to a lightly floured surface. Form the dough into a circle about ½-inch thick. With a long knife, cut the dough into 12 wedges.

5 Butter a cast-iron Dutch oven then place the scone wedges in a circle, leaving some space between the pieces. When the coals are glowing, cover and bake for 20 to 25 minutes, or until golden, turning the Dutch oven every few minutes to avoid burn spots.

Cheddar & Jalapeño Scones

YIELD: 4 TO 6 SERVINGS • ACTIVE TIME: 30 MINUTES • TOTAL TIME: 50 MINUTES

The spiciness of jalapeño livens up any meal. For an added kick of flavor, split the cooked scones in half and put a spoonful of sour cream and some sliced avocado in the middle.

INGREDIENTS

2 CUPS ALL-PURPOSE FLOUR, PLUS MORE FOR DUSTING

1 TEASPOON BAKING POWDER

½ TEASPOON SALT

1 TEASPOON FRESHLY GROUND BLACK PEPPER

4 TABLESPOONS UNSALTED BUTTER, CHILLED, CUT INTO PIECES

¾ CUP GRATED SHARP CHEDDAR CHEESE

½ CUP SLICED OR CHOPPED JALAPEÑO PEPPER

½ CUP WHOLE MILK

1 EGG, BEATEN WITH A LITTLE MILK

DIRECTIONS

1 Position a grate over the fire using gloved hands and tongs. Make sure the grate is as secure and level as possible.

2 In a large bowl, whisk together the flour, baking powder, salt, and black pepper. Add the butter pieces and mix with a fork so that the dough is somewhat crumbly.

3 Stir in the cheese, jalapeño, and milk, being careful not to overmix.

4 With flour on your hands, transfer the dough to a lightly floured surface. Form the dough into a circle about ½-inch thick. With a long knife, cut the dough into 12 wedges.

5 Place the wedges in a circle in a lightly greased cast-iron Dutch oven, leaving some space between the pieces.

6 Brush with the beaten egg. When the coals are glowing, bake for 20 to 25 minutes, or until golden, turning the Dutch oven every few minutes to prevent burn spots.

VARIATION: Ramp up the heat by substituting Pepper Jack cheese for the cheddar, or substitute a serrano pepper for the jalapeño.

Cornmeal Crepes

YIELD: 6 SERVINGS • ACTIVE TIME: 40 MINUTES • TOTAL TIME: 1 HOUR AND 20 MINUTES

These crepes put a French twist on the traditional johnnycake. You can fill them with almost anything, but they're particularly wonderful with fruit and real maple syrup.

INGREDIENTS

¾ CUP FINELY GROUND CORNMEAL

1¼ CUPS ALL-PURPOSE FLOUR

1 TEASPOON SALT

1 TEASPOON CINNAMON

1¾ CUPS WHOLE MILK

¼ CUP CREAM

3 EGGS

4 TABLESPOONS MELTED UNSALTED BUTTER, PLUS MORE AS NEEDED

DIRECTIONS

1 Position a grate over the fire using gloved hands and tongs. Make sure the grate is as secure and level as possible.

2 Sift the cornmeal, flour, salt, and cinnamon into a bowl.

3 Place the milk, cream, eggs, and 3 tablespoons of the butter in another bowl and beat until combined. Add the wet mixture to the dry mixture, stir to combine, and let stand for 30 to 40 minutes.

4 When the coals are glowing, place a 10-inch cast-iron skillet on the grate and add the remaining butter. Stir the batter and pour about ⅓ cup into the skillet. Tilt and swirl the pan so that a thin layer of the batter covers the entirety of it.

5 Cook until the edges of the crepe start to lift away from the pan and turn slightly golden. Turn the crepe over and cook for another 20 to 30 seconds. Transfer cooked crepes to a plate and cover. If the skillet becomes too dry, add butter as needed.

Campfire French Toast

YIELD: 4 TO 6 SERVINGS • ACTIVE TIME: 20 MINUTES • TOTAL TIME: 40 MINUTES

The secret to great French toast is the choice of bread and the amount of egg mixture that saturates the bread. If you use a basic sandwich bread, you won't need as much egg mixture. If you use an egg-based bread like challah, or a sourdough bread, you'll need more egg mixture, as these kinds of bread are denser. They will also need to sit in the egg mixture longer. As you'll need to adjust the recipe for the type of bread you're using, make sure to have some extra eggs and milk on hand.

INGREDIENTS

6 EGGS

1 CUP WHOLE MILK

½ TEASPOON VANILLA EXTRACT

PINCH OF NUTMEG (OPTIONAL)

6 THICK-CUT SLICES OF BREAD

4-6 TABLESPOONS UNSALTED BUTTER

MAPLE SYRUP, FOR SERVING (OPTIONAL)

JAM, FOR SERVING (OPTIONAL)

DIRECTIONS

1 Position a grate over the fire using gloved hands and tongs. Make sure the grate is as secure and level as possible.

2 In a mixing bowl, combine the eggs, milk, vanilla, and nutmeg (if desired).

3 Place the slices of bread in a baking dish. Pour the egg mixture over the bread, shaking the pan to distribute evenly. Flip the pieces of bread a couple of times to coat both sides with the mixture.

4 When the coals are glowing, place a 10-inch cast-iron skillet on the grate and heat 2 tablespoons of the butter. Add 2 slices of bread to the skillet and cook until golden brown on each side, 2 to 3 minutes a side. Transfer the cooked pieces to a warm plate or keep warm on the outer edges of the grate while you cook the additional pieces.

5 Serve with maple syrup or jam.

VARIATION: If you want to make gluten-free French toast, just use gluten-free bread. It's as simple and delicious as that. You'll want one that's got some density to it and minimal crust.

Pecan-Crusted Maple French Toast

YIELD: 4 SERVINGS • ACTIVE TIME: 20 MINUTES • TOTAL TIME: 40 MINUTES

What better to do with leftover crusty bread than soak it in some fresh eggs and cream, sizzle it up in some butter, and encase it in pecans and maple syrup? Enjoying it with strong coffee and thick-sliced bacon, that's what!

INGREDIENTS

4 EGGS

½ CUP HEAVY CREAM

¾ CUP ALL-NATURAL MAPLE SYRUP, PLUS MORE TO TASTE

8 SLICES OF SLIGHTLY STALE THICK-CUT BREAD

2 CUPS PECANS, FINELY CHOPPED

1 TEASPOON CINNAMON

1 TEASPOON NUTMEG

4 TABLESPOONS UNSALTED BUTTER

DIRECTIONS

1 Position a grate over the fire using gloved hands and tongs. Make sure the grate is as secure and level as possible.

2 In a small bowl, combine the eggs, heavy cream, and ½ cup of the maple syrup. Whisk to thoroughly combine.

3 Put the bread in a dish and cover with the egg mixture. Let the bread soak up the egg mixture for about 20 minutes, turning halfway so both sides can soak.

4 Place the chopped pecans, cinnamon, and nutmeg in a shallow dish and stir before spreading out across the dish. Dip each slice of soaked bread into the pecan-spice mixture, making sure every slice is covered on both sides.

5 When the coals are glowing, place a 10-inch cast-iron skillet over the grate. Add 2 tablespoons of the butter and, as it melts, tilt the pan to coat it evenly. When the butter is heated but not browned, add 4 slices of the pecan-crusted bread. Allow to cook for about 4 minutes, then flip. Drizzle the pieces with maple syrup while they're cooking on the other side, and after another 4 minutes or so, flip them again so the side with the maple syrup gets cooked for about 1 minute.

Continued...

6 Transfer the cooked pieces to the outer edges of the grate to keep warm. Repeat the cooking process for the remaining slices of bread.

7 Before serving, warm the remaining maple syrup (and some additional syrup) in a container. Test the warmth. You don't want to over-warm it, just take the chill out. Serve the French toast with maple syrup.

TIP: The sugar in the maple syrup will also caramelize on the skillet as long as the heat is not too hot, which will toast the sugar without burning it.

Skillet Apple Pancake

YIELD: 4 TO 6 SERVINGS • ACTIVE TIME: 30 MINUTES • TOTAL TIME: 1 HOUR

Make this with fresh apples to get your day off to a great start.

INGREDIENTS

4 EGGS

1 CUP WHOLE MILK

3 TABLESPOONS SUGAR

½ TEASPOON VANILLA EXTRACT

½ TEASPOON SALT

¾ CUP ALL-PURPOSE FLOUR

4 TABLESPOONS UNSALTED BUTTER

2 APPLES, PEELED, CORED, AND SLICED THIN

¼ TEASPOON CINNAMON

DASH OF GROUND NUTMEG

DASH OF GROUND GINGER

¼ CUP LIGHT BROWN SUGAR

CONFECTIONERS' SUGAR, FOR SPRINKLING (OPTIONAL)

DIRECTIONS

1 Position a grate over the fire using gloved hands and tongs. Make sure the grate is as secure and level as possible.

2 In a large bowl, whisk together the eggs, milk, sugar, vanilla, and salt. Add the flour and whisk to combine. Set the batter aside.

3 When the coals are glowing, place a 12-inch cast-iron skillet on the grate and add the butter, tilting the pan to thoroughly coat the bottom. Add the apple slices and top with the cinnamon, nutmeg, and ginger. Cook, while stirring, until apples begin to soften, about 5 minutes. Add the brown sugar and continue to stir while cooking for an additional few minutes, until the apples are very soft. Pat the cooked apples along the bottom of the skillet to distribute evenly.

4 Pour the batter over the apples, coating them evenly. Cover and bake for about 20 minutes, turning the skillet every few minutes to avoid burn spots. When the pancake is browned and puffy, remove from the heat and sprinkle with confectioners' sugar, if desired. Serve immediately.

VARIATION: To make a gluten-free version of this recipe, just substitute the ¾ cup of flour with ¾ cup Gluten Free All-Purpose Baking Flour from Bob's Red Mill and add 1 teaspoon of xanthan gum. Mix together before whisking into your wet ingredients.

David Eyre's Pancake

YIELD: 4 SERVINGS • ACTIVE TIME: 30 MINUTES • TOTAL TIME: 30 MINUTES

This recipe was run in the *New York Times* years ago and has quite the following. It's more of a popover than a traditional pancake, but it's a delicious tribute to writer and editor David Eyre.

INGREDIENTS

½ CUP ALL-PURPOSE FLOUR

½ CUP WHOLE MILK

2 EGGS, LIGHTLY BEATEN

PINCH OF NUTMEG

4 TABLESPOONS UNSALTED BUTTER

2 TABLESPOONS CONFECTIONERS' SUGAR

JUICE OF ½ LEMON

JAM, FOR SERVING

DIRECTIONS

1 Position a grate over the fire using gloved hands and tongs. Make sure the grate is as secure and level as possible.

2 In a bowl, combine the flour, milk, eggs, and nutmeg. Beat lightly; leave the batter a little lumpy.

3 Melt the butter in a 12-inch cast-iron skillet and move the skillet closer to the center of the fire. When very hot, pour in the batter.

4 Cover and bake for 15 to 20 minutes, until golden brown, turning the skillet every few minutes to avoid burn spots.

5 Sprinkle with the sugar, warm briefly, then remove. Sprinkle with lemon juice and serve with your favorite jam.

Whole Grain Porridge

YIELD: 4 SERVINGS • ACTIVE TIME: 5 MINUTES • TOTAL TIME: 30 MINUTES

This dish is all about mastering the method and then tweaking to make it your own. Try this recipe as suggested, and then take all of the liberties you can think of, swapping in any grain, dried fruit, and milk that you want.

INGREDIENTS

1 CUP BUCKWHEAT GROATS

1 CUP STEEL-CUT OATS

2 TABLESPOONS FLAX SEEDS

2 TEASPOONS CINNAMON

1 CUP CHOPPED DRIED FRUIT (APPLES, APRICOTS, PINEAPPLE, DATES, ETC.)

2 CUPS WATER

2 CUPS ALMOND MILK

1 GRANNY SMITH APPLE, FOR GARNISH

¼ CUP CHOPPED ALMONDS, FOR GARNISH

DIRECTIONS

1 Position a grate over the fire using gloved hands and tongs. Make sure the grate is as secure and level as possible.

2 Place all of the ingredients, other than the Granny Smith apple and the almonds, in a cast-iron Dutch oven.

3 Bring to a gentle simmer and cover. Cook, while stirring occasionally to prevent the porridge from sticking to the bottom, for 20 minutes. Turn the Dutch oven every few minutes to avoid burn spots.

4 Remove the porridge from heat and ladle into warm bowls. Peel the apple and grate it over each bowl. Top with the chopped almonds and serve.

Campfire Grits

YIELD: 8 TO 10 SERVINGS • ACTIVE TIME: 15 MINUTES • TOTAL TIME: 45 MINUTES

The beauty of cast iron is on full display with the grits, as it lends the bottom a gorgeous burnish.

INGREDIENTS

4 CUPS WATER

1 CUP QUICK-COOKING GRITS

2 LARGE EGGS

4 TABLESPOONS UNSALTED BUTTER, AT ROOM TEMPERATURE

¾ CUP WHOLE MILK

SALT AND PEPPER, TO TASTE

1 LB. CHEDDAR CHEESE, GRATED

DIRECTIONS

1 Position a grate over the fire using gloved hands and tongs. Make sure the grate is as secure and level as possible.

2 Place the water in a saucepan and bring to a boil. While stirring constantly, slowly add the grits. Cover, move the saucepan to the edge of the grate, and cook, while stirring occasionally, until the grits are quite thick, about 5 minutes. Remove from heat.

3 Place the eggs, butter, and milk in a bowl, season with salt and pepper, and stir to combine. Stir the cooked grits into the egg mixture, add three-quarters of the cheese, and stir to incorporate.

4 Pour the mixture into a greased cast-iron Dutch oven, cover, and bake for 30 minutes, turning the Dutch oven every few minutes to avoid burn spots. Remove from heat, sprinkle the remaining cheese on top, and return the grits to the heat. Bake until the cheese is melted and the grits are firm, about 15 minutes. Remove from heat and let cool slightly before cutting into squares and serving.

Peanut Butter & Bacon Oats with Fried Eggs

YIELD: 4 TO 6 SERVINGS • ACTIVE TIME: 5 MINUTES • TOTAL TIME: 20 MINUTES

Peanut butter, bacon, and eggs in oats? It may sound crazy at first, but the saltiness of the crispy bacon, the texture added by the peanut butter, and the creaminess of the egg yolk work really well together, creating a brand-new take on oatmeal.

INGREDIENTS

6 SLICES OF THICK-CUT BACON

6 EGGS

2 CUPS OATS

6 CUPS WATER

1 TABLESPOON KOSHER SALT

¼ CUP PEANUT BUTTER OF YOUR CHOICE

DIRECTIONS

1 Position a grate over the fire using gloved hands and tongs. Make sure the grate is as secure and level as possible.

2 When the coals are glowing, cook the bacon in a 10-inch cast-iron skillet. Remove the bacon from the skillet and use the bacon fat to fry the eggs.

3 When the eggs have been fried, remove them from the skillet and set aside. Wipe remaining grease from the skillet with a paper towel. Add oats, water, and salt and cook for 7 to 10 minutes, or until oats are the desired consistency.

4 While the oats are cooking, chop the bacon. Add the bacon and peanut butter to the oatmeal and stir to combine.

5 Top each portion with a fried egg and serve.

Huevos Rancheros

YIELD: 4 SERVINGS • ACTIVE TIME: 25 MINUTES • TOTAL TIME: 40 MINUTES

You can make this a one-dish meal by cutting the tortillas into ½-inch pieces and frying them. Once they've crisped up, spoon the beans and butter over them, pressing them into the bottom of the skillet to brown. Break the eggs over the beans and cover so that the eggs start to set. Cook for about 2 minutes. Take off the lid, cover with cheese, and serve.

INGREDIENTS

2 TABLESPOONS VEGETABLE OIL

4 CORN TORTILLAS (SEE PAGE 80)

½ LB. BLACK OR REFRIED BEANS

1 TABLESPOON UNSALTED BUTTER

4 EGGS

½ CUP GRATED SHARP CHEDDAR CHEESE

½ CUP COTIJA OR GRATED MONTEREY JACK CHEESE

½ CUP FRESH SALSA, FOR SERVING

JALAPEÑO PEPPERS, SLICED, FOR SERVING

FRESH CILANTRO, CHOPPED, FOR SERVING

DIRECTIONS

1 Position a grate over the fire using gloved hands and tongs. Make sure the grate is as secure and level as possible.

2 When the coals are glowing, heat the oil in a 10-inch cast-iron skillet. Fry the tortillas, one at a time, until firm but not crisp. Transfer cooked tortillas to a plate lined with a paper towel, and separate with paper towels while cooking.

3 Put the beans and butter in a bowl and heat on the side of the grate for about 1 minute, stirring halfway through.

4 Fry the eggs in the skillet over easy and, once nearly cooked, sprinkle with cheese so that the cheese melts.

5 Place a crispy tortilla on a plate, top with the beans and eggs, and serve hot with the salsa, jalapeños, and cilantro.

Steak & Pearl Onion Frittata

YIELD: 6 SERVINGS • ACTIVE TIME: 10 MINUTES • TOTAL TIME: 25 MINUTES

Frittatas are traditionally enjoyed at breakfast, but this one is hearty enough to work any time of day. Serve this with an arugula-and-red onion salad for a quick on-the-go lunch if you find yourself pressed for time.

INGREDIENTS

2 TABLESPOONS OLIVE OIL

1 LB. PEARL ONIONS

SALT AND PEPPER, TO TASTE

12 LARGE EGGS

½ CUP HEAVY CREAM OR HALF-AND-HALF

1 (7 TO 8 OZ.) STRIP STEAK, MINCED

4 TABLESPOONS UNSALTED BUTTER

2 TABLESPOONS CHOPPED FRESH PARSLEY

2 CUPS SHREDDED PARMESAN OR ASIAGO CHEESE

DIRECTIONS

1 Position a grate over the fire using gloved hands and tongs. Make sure the grate is as secure and level as possible.

2 When the coals are glowing, place a cast-iron Dutch oven on the grate and add the olive oil. Once the Dutch oven is hot, add the pearl onions, salt, and pepper and cook until onions start to caramelize, about 5 to 7 minutes.

3 While the onions are cooking, place the eggs, cream or half-and-half, salt, and pepper in a bowl and scramble until combined.

4 Add the steak to the Dutch oven with the onions and cook until the steak is cooked through, about 4 to 5 minutes. Add the butter and parsley and stir until the butter is melted. Sprinkle the cheese evenly over the onions and steak, then pour the egg mixture into the Dutch oven. The eggs should just cover everything else in the pot. Cover the Dutch oven and cook for 15-20 minutes, turning the Dutch oven every few minutes to avoid burn spots. When the top of the frittata is brown, remove from heat and serve.

Tamagoyaki

YIELD: 2 SERVINGS • ACTIVE TIME: 15 MINUTES • TOTAL TIME: 15 MINUTES

This is a sweet-and-savory Japanese omelette that is traditionally made in a small rectangular pan. It takes a bit of practice to get just right, but once you master it, you'll find yourself making it all the time. It's equally good warm, cold, or in a sushi roll.

INGREDIENTS

4 LARGE EGGS

¼ TEASPOON KOSHER SALT

1 TEASPOON SOY SAUCE

1 TABLESPOON MIRIN

1 TABLESPOON VEGETABLE OIL

DIRECTIONS

1 Position a grate over the fire using gloved hands and tongs. Make sure the grate is as secure and level as possible.

2 Place the eggs, salt, soy sauce, and mirin in a bowl and whisk to combine.

3 When the coals are glowing, place the vegetable oil in a rectangular cast-iron pan and warm.

4 Pour a thin layer of the egg mixture into the pan, tilting and swirling to make sure the egg completely coats the bottom. When the bottom of the egg is just set and there is still liquid on top, use a chopstick to gently roll the egg up into a log. If you allow the egg to cook too much, it won't stick as you roll it.

5 When the first roll is at one end of the pan, pour another thin layer of egg mixture into the pan. When the bottom of this layer is set, roll the log back onto it. Roll the layer up to the other end of the pan. Repeat until all of the egg mixture has been used up.

6 Remove the omelette from the pan and let it set for a few minutes before trimming the ends and slicing into even pieces.

Chicken Sausage Hash

YIELD: 4 TO 6 SERVINGS • ACTIVE TIME: 15 MINUTES • TOTAL TIME: 30 MINUTES

You can follow this recipe step-by-step and have breakfast on the table in a half hour. Or you can cook the sausage and potatoes the night before, start with Step 3, and have it ready in a flash. Serve this with hot sauce, salsa, or maple syrup.

INGREDIENTS

¼ CUP OLIVE OIL

2 LARGE LINKS OF SPICY CHICKEN SAUSAGE

2 YUKON GOLD POTATOES, DICED INTO ½-INCH CUBES

SALT AND PEPPER, TO TASTE

1 YELLOW ONION, DICED

6 EGGS

DIRECTIONS

1 Position a grate over the fire using gloved hands and tongs. Make sure the grate is as secure and level as possible.

2 When the coals are glowing, warm a 12-inch cast-iron skillet and add 2 tablespoons of the oil. When the oil is shimmering, add the chicken sausage and cook until browned all over, about 8 minutes. Remove the sausage from the skillet and set aside. When cool enough to handle, chop the sausage into bite-sized pieces.

3 Add the remaining oil to the skillet. When the oil is shimmering, add the potatoes, season with salt and pepper, and cook until browned. Cover the pan and let steam for 5 minutes.

4 Remove the lid, add the onion, and cook, while stirring occasionally, until the onion is browned, about 5 minutes.

5 Gently fold in the chopped sausage and continue to cook until the potatoes are fork-tender, about 10 minutes.

6 Using a large spoon, press down on the hash and then make six indentations. Crack an egg into each indentation. Cover the skillet and cook until the egg whites are firm, about 5 minutes. Serve immediately.

Corned Beef Hash

YIELD: 4 SERVINGS • ACTIVE TIME: 15 MINUTES • TOTAL TIME: 35 MINUTES

Start your day off right with this hearty breakfast hash. The recipe originated in the 1950s and the name comes from the French word *hacher*, which means "to chop." If roast beef is easier to come by than corned beef, feel free to use that.

INGREDIENTS

5 TABLESPOONS VEGETABLE OIL

2 YUKON GOLD POTATOES, DICED INTO ¼-INCH CUBES

1 YELLOW ONION, SLICED INTO THIN HALF-MOONS

1 RED OR GREEN BELL PEPPER, SEEDED AND SLICED THIN

1½ LBS. COOKED CORNED BEEF, DICED

1 CUP TOMATO SAUCE

2 TABLESPOONS TOMATO PASTE

1 TEASPOON HOT SAUCE

4 LARGE EGGS

CHIVES, CHOPPED, FOR GARNISH

DIRECTIONS

1 Position a grate over the fire using gloved hands and tongs. Make sure the grate is as secure and level as possible.

2 When the coals are glowing, place 3 tablespoons of the vegetable oil in a 12-inch cast-iron skillet. When the oil is shimmering, add the potatoes and cook, while stirring occasionally, until they are golden brown, about 10 minutes.

3 Shift the skillet away from the center of the fire and add the onion and bell pepper. Cook, while stirring occasionally, for 2 minutes. Add the corned beef and cook until browned, about 8 minutes. Pour in the tomato sauce, tomato paste, and hot sauce, stir to coat, and allow the hash to simmer, while stirring occasionally, for 15 minutes.

4 While the hash is simmering, place the remaining vegetable oil in another cast-iron skillet. When the oil is shimmering, crack the eggs into the skillet and cook until the whites are cooked through. To cut down on dishes, you can also make four indentations in the hash, crack the eggs into them, and cook until the whites are set.

5 To serve, spoon the hash onto plates and top each portion with a fried egg. Sprinkle the chives on top and serve immediately.

Cheesy Hash Browns

YIELD: 4 TO 6 SERVINGS • ACTIVE TIME: 20 MINUTES • TOTAL TIME: 1 HOUR

If you want gooey goodness, this recipe is for you. Be careful not to overcook it or you'll go from gooey to overly chewy. The best cheeses to use in this recipe are those that melt well, like cheddar, Swiss, American, mozzarella, Monterey Jack, or Provolone.

INGREDIENTS

4 TABLESPOONS UNSALTED BUTTER

4 LARGE RUSSET POTATOES, SHREDDED WITH A CHEESE GRATER AND SQUEEZED DRY

1 TEASPOON SALT

½ TEASPOON FRESHLY GROUND BLACK PEPPER, OR TO TASTE

6 EGGS

½ CUP WHOLE MILK

1 CUP SHREDDED CHEESE

DIRECTIONS

1 Position a grate over the fire using gloved hands and tongs. Make sure the grate is as secure and level as possible.

2 When the coals are glowing, add the butter to a Dutch oven. When the butter starts to foam, add the potatoes and season with the salt and pepper. Press the potatoes into the bottom of the Dutch oven. Cook for about 5 minutes.

3 In a mixing bowl, whisk the eggs and milk together. Pour the eggs over the potatoes, shaking the Dutch oven to help them penetrate to the bottom. Sprinkle liberally with the cheese.

4 Cover the Dutch oven and cook, turning the Dutch oven every few minutes to avoid burn spots, until just set, about 10 minutes. Serve immediately.

SIDES & STARCHES

The delicious sides in this chapter show that just about anything is suited for cooking in cast iron. That's what makes your cast-iron skillet or Dutch oven your best companion at the campsite.

Campfire Roasted Potatoes

YIELD: 4 TO 6 SERVINGS • ACTIVE TIME: 5 MINUTES • TOTAL TIME: 1 HOUR

A classic side dish, made even better thanks to a little browning and crisping in a cast-iron pan. If you'd like to spice this up a little bit, try adding a pinch of cayenne pepper during the last 5 minutes of cooking.

INGREDIENTS

2½ LBS. RED OR FINGERLING POTATOES

2 TABLESPOONS OLIVE OIL

1 TEASPOON KOSHER SALT

FRESHLY GROUND BLACK PEPPER, TO TASTE

DIRECTIONS

1 Position a grate over the fire using gloved hands and tongs. Make sure the grate is as secure and level as possible.

2 If using red potatoes, cut them in half.

3 When the coals are glowing, place a 12-inch cast-iron skillet on the grate to warm.

4 Place the potatoes, olive oil, salt, and pepper in a bowl and toss to coat.

5 Arrange the potatoes in a single layer in the skillet and cook for 10 minutes, while stirring occasionally.

6 Cover the pan, move further from the center of the fire, and cook until the potatoes are fork-tender, about 30 minutes, turning the skillet every few minutes to avoid burn spots.

Potato & Tomato Gratin

YIELD: 4 TO 6 SERVINGS • ACTIVE TIME: 15 MINUTES • TOTAL TIME: 45 MINUTES

A testament to the brilliance of French cuisine, this layered dish has all the flavor in the world and is as simple as can be to make. Try serving it with grilled chicken and sautéed kohlrabi.

INGREDIENTS

4 GARLIC CLOVES, MINCED

LEAVES FROM 1 SMALL BUNCH OF PARSLEY, MINCED

2 TABLESPOONS MINCED FRESH THYME LEAVES

OLIVE OIL, TO TASTE

2 LBS. TOMATOES, SLICED ¼-INCH THICK

SALT AND PEPPER, TO TASTE

4 WAXY POTATOES, SLICED ¼-INCH THICK

CHICKEN STOCK, AS NEEDED

DIRECTIONS

1 Position a grate over the fire using gloved hands and tongs. Make sure the grate is as secure and level as possible.

2 Place the garlic, parsley, and thyme in a small bowl, stir to combine, and set it aside while you prepare the tomatoes.

3 Lightly oil a cast-iron Dutch oven and then add a layer of the tomato slices. Season with salt and pepper and add a layer of potatoes and a sprinkle of the garlic-and-parsley mixture. Drizzle with olive oil and continue the layering process until all of the tomatoes, potatoes, and garlic-and-parsley mixture have been used.

4 When the coals are glowing, cover with foil and bake for 20 minutes, turning the Dutch oven every few minutes to avoid burn spots. Remove from the heat and remove the foil. If tomatoes haven't released enough liquid to soften the potatoes, add a bit of the stock. Replace the foil and continue baking for 15 minutes.

5 Remove the foil, cook for an additional 5 minutes, and serve warm.

Zucchini Fritters with Sumac Yogurt

YIELD: 4 SERVINGS • ACTIVE TIME: 15 MINUTES • TOTAL TIME: 30 MINUTES

Zucchini has a number of wonderful uses, and turning it into fritters is one of the easiest ways to get people excited about this summer squash. Staghorn sumac is native to the eastern United States, but its citric quality is massively underutilized outside of Middle Eastern cuisine. That is, until you try this recipe.

INGREDIENTS

1½ LBS. ZUCCHINI

SALT AND PEPPER, TO TASTE

¼ CUP ALL-PURPOSE FLOUR

¼ CUP GRATED PARMESAN CHEESE

1 EGG, BEATEN

3 TABLESPOONS CANOLA OIL

1 CUP YOGURT

2 TEASPOONS FRESH LEMON JUICE

2 TABLESPOONS SUMAC POWDER

DIRECTIONS

1 Position a grate over the fire using gloved hands and tongs. Make sure the grate is as secure and level as possible.

2 Grate the zucchini into a large bowl. Line a colander with cheesecloth and then place the grated zucchini in the colander, salt it, and let stand for 1 hour. Then press down to remove as much water from the zucchini as you can.

3 Place the zucchini, flour, Parmesan, and egg in a mixing bowl and stir to combine.

4 Use your hands to form handfuls of the mixture into balls and then gently press down on the balls to form them into patties.

5 When the coals are glowing, place the canola oil in a 12-inch cast-iron skillet.

6 Working in batches, place the patties into the oil, taking care not to crowd the skillet. Cook until golden brown, about 5 minutes. Flip them over and cook, until the fritters are also golden brown on that side, another 5 minutes. Remove from the skillet and drain on a paper towel–lined plate.

7 Place the yogurt, lemon juice, and sumac powder in a small bowl and stir to combine.

8 Season the fritters with salt and pepper and serve the yogurt mixture on the side.

Home-Style Baked Beans

YIELD: 6 TO 8 SERVINGS • ACTIVE TIME: 30 MINUTES • TOTAL TIME: 1½ TO 2 HOURS

At times, cooking in a cast-iron Dutch oven or skillet makes you picture cowboys cooking over an open fire while their horses hang out behind them, and nothing is more quintessential to cast-iron cooking than baked beans. Baked beans are delicious and filling on their own, but they are the perfect accompaniment to grilled sausages, hot dogs, hamburgers, pork chops, or barbecued chicken.

INGREDIENTS

6 SLICES OF THICK-CUT BACON

½ ONION, DICED

½ CUP DICED BELL PEPPER

1 TEASPOON SALT, PLUS MORE TO TASTE

2 (14 OZ.) CANS OF PINTO BEANS, RINSED AND DRAINED

1 CUP BARBECUE SAUCE

1 TEASPOON DIJON MUSTARD

2 TABLESPOONS DARK BROWN SUGAR

FRESHLY GROUND BLACK PEPPER, TO TASTE

DIRECTIONS

1 Position a grate over the fire using gloved hands and tongs. Make sure the grate is as secure and level as possible. If using a tripod, set up prior to building your fire. You will need a round bottomed cauldron or a Dutch oven with a hanging loop handle.

2 When the coals are glowing, heat a cast-iron Dutch oven or a hanging cast-iron Dutch oven and cook half of the bacon slices until just soft, about 8 minutes. Transfer to a paper towel–lined plate to drain.

3 Add the remaining slices of bacon, move closer to the center of the fire, and cook, flipping often, until browned. Move the Dutch oven further from the center of the fire. Add the onion and bell pepper and cook, stirring occasionally, until the vegetables soften, another 8 minutes or so.

4 Add the salt, beans, barbecue sauce, mustard, and brown sugar. Stir, season with additional salt and a generous grind of fresh pepper, and leave over the fire until the sauce just starts to simmer.

5 Lay the partially cooked pieces of bacon on top of the beans and cover the Dutch oven.

6 Bake, turning the Dutch oven every few minutes to avoid burn spots, for 1 hour and check. The bacon should be crisp and browned, and the sauce should be thick. The dish can cook for another 15 to 30 minutes if the consistency isn't right. Be careful not to overcook, as the beans will start to dry out.

7 Remove from heat and allow to cool slightly before serving.

Quinoa Skillet Casserole

YIELD: 6 SERVINGS • ACTIVE TIME: 30 MINUTES • TOTAL TIME: 1 HOUR

Quinoa looks and cooks like a grain, but it's actually a seed that has grown in the Andes Mountains of South America for millennia. It's high in protein and fiber and loaded with magnesium, iron, and vitamin B6. Quinoa has plenty of health benefits, but one of the drawbacks of this nutritious food is that it can become sticky, like oatmeal—a texture that isn't always appealing. With the cast-iron skillet, you can cook the quinoa so that it gets almost crackly-crunchy. Combined with the veggies and hot peppers, this is a delish dish.

INGREDIENTS

1 CUP QUINOA

2 CUPS CHICKEN BROTH

1½ TABLESPOONS OLIVE OIL

KERNELS FROM 1 EAR OF COOKED CORN

½ RED BELL PEPPER, SEEDED AND DICED

½ CUP CHOPPED YELLOW ONION

1 JALAPEÑO PEPPER, SEEDED AND SLICED

½ TEASPOON SALT

1 CUP GRATED CHEDDAR CHEESE

DIRECTIONS

1 Position a grate over the fire using gloved hands and tongs. Make sure the grate is as secure and level as possible.

2 When the coals are glowing, place the quinoa and the broth in a small saucepan with a tight-fitting lid. Bring to a boil, stir, cover, and move further from the center of the fire, simmering for about 15 minutes or until the grains are translucent. Remove from heat and let sit, still covered, for at least 5 more minutes so the quinoa fully absorbs the broth.

3 Place a 12-inch cast-iron skillet on the grate, add the olive oil, and then add the corn, red pepper, onion, and jalapeño. Stir, cooking, until the onion is soft and the peppers are starting to brown, about 5 to 8 minutes.

4 Stir in the quinoa, season with salt, and cook to brown the quinoa slightly.

5 Cook for another 10 minutes, while stirring occasionally. Stir in the cheese, remove from heat, and serve.

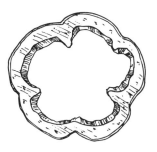

Polenta Cake with Mushrooms & Onions

YIELD: 4 TO 6 SERVINGS • ACTIVE TIME: 30 MINUTES • TOTAL TIME: 1 HOUR AND 15 MINUTES

Think vegetarian shepherd's pie with this recipe—the mushrooms and onions are the "meat" and the polenta bakes on top the way a layer of mashed potatoes would. A cast-iron Dutch oven is a natural home for this hearty and rustic dish.

INGREDIENTS

1 STICK OF UNSALTED BUTTER

1-1½ CUPS THINLY SLICED ONIONS

2 LBS. MUSHROOMS, STEMMED AND CHOPPED

1 TEASPOON WORCESTERSHIRE SAUCE

SALT AND PEPPER, TO TASTE

1 CUP POLENTA

3 CUPS WATER

DIRECTIONS

1 Position a grate over the fire using gloved hands and tongs. Make sure the grate is as secure and level as possible.

2 When the coals are glowing, melt 6 tablespoons of the butter in a cast-iron Dutch oven. Add the onion slices and move the Dutch oven closer to the center of the fire. Sauté the onions until just soft, about 3 minutes. Add the mushroom pieces and continue to cook, while stirring frequently, until the mushrooms and onions are soft and reduced in volume, about 8 minutes. Stir in the Worcestershire sauce and season with salt and pepper. Remove the Dutch oven from the heat.

3 In a heavy saucepan, whisk together the polenta and water. Bring to a boil, whisking to prevent lumps from forming. When bubbling, move the pan to the edge of the fire and simmer, uncovered, for a couple of minutes or until smooth. Season with salt and pepper.

4 Pour the polenta over the mushroom-and-onion mixture, smoothing the surface with the back of a spoon. Cut the remaining 2 tablespoons of butter into thin pieces and dot the surface of the polenta with them.

5 Cover the Dutch oven and bake, turning the Dutch oven every few minutes to avoid burn spots, for 30 minutes, until it is lightly golden and coming away from the edges of the pot (the filling should be bubbling hot). Allow to cool for 10 minutes before serving.

6 Cut into wedges and serve immediately.

Dutch Oven Mac & Cheese

YIELD: 6 TO 8 SERVINGS • ACTIVE TIME: 30 MINUTES • TOTAL TIME: 1 HOUR

There's nothing like homemade macaroni and cheese, but it can get messy when you have to use several pots and pans to make and serve it. Here comes your cast iron to the rescue!

INGREDIENTS

1 LB. ELBOW MACARONI OR PREFERRED PASTA

1 TABLESPOON SALT

3 TABLESPOONS UNSALTED BUTTER, AT ROOM TEMPERATURE

3½ TABLESPOONS ALL-PURPOSE FLOUR

1½ CUPS WHOLE MILK, AT ROOM TEMPERATURE OR SLIGHTLY WARMED

¼ CUP SOUR CREAM

¾ LB. SHARP WHITE CHEDDAR CHEESE, GRATED

¼ LB. GRUYÈRE CHEESE, GRATED

SALT AND PEPPER, TO TASTE

DASH OF CAYENNE PEPPER

DIRECTIONS

1 Position a grate over the fire using gloved hands and tongs. Make sure the grate is as secure and level as possible.

2 When the coals are glowing, put the macaroni in a cast-iron Dutch oven and add cold water. Stir in the salt and cook the macaroni for about 10 minutes. Test a piece after about 7 minutes. The pasta should be al dente—nearly cooked through but still a bit chewy. When it is cooked, drain it in a colander over a large mixing bowl so the water is retained.

3 Put your Dutch oven back over the fire and add the butter. When it's melted, stir in the flour, with a wooden spoon if possible, to prevent lumps from forming. When it is starting to bubble, start slowly adding the milk, whisking constantly as you add it. Add about ½ cup at a time, being sure to whisk it in thoroughly before continuing. When all the milk is stirred in, let the sauce simmer until thickened, about 10 minutes.

4 Move the sauce further from the center of the fire and stir in the sour cream. When the mix is warm again, add the cheeses, stirring gently as they melt. Season with the salt, pepper, and cayenne.

5 Finally, add the macaroni gently into the cheese sauce. If it seems too thick, add some of the reserved water. The consistency should be like a thick stew. When the noodles are hot, cover the Dutch oven.

6 Bake for about 15 minutes, turning every few minutes to avoid burn spots, then check. The dish should be bubbling and the cheese on top starting to brown. This takes somewhere between 15 and 25 minutes. Let the macaroni cool slightly before serving.

Noodles & Cabbage

YIELD: 6 TO 8 SERVINGS • ACTIVE TIME: 30 MINUTES • TOTAL TIME: 2 HOURS AND 30 MINUTES

A deceptive dish: it only has five ingredients, and yet it is the ultimate comfort food. If you're committed to making it, know that the longer you cook the cabbage, the sweeter it becomes.

INGREDIENTS

1½ STICKS OF SALTED BUTTER, DIVIDED INTO TABLESPOONS

2 HEADS OF GREEN CABBAGE, CORED AND SLICED AS THIN AS POSSIBLE

SALT AND WHITE PEPPER, TO TASTE

1 LB. WIDE EGG NOODLES

DIRECTIONS

1 Position a grate over the fire using gloved hands and tongs. Make sure the grate is as secure and level as possible.

2 When the coals are glowing, place half of the butter in a large cast-iron Dutch oven and melt it.

3 Add the cabbage. If it doesn't fit initially, push down what does fit in the pot and add more as that wilts. Cover with a lid and cook for 10 minutes.

4 Remove the lid and add the remaining butter. Cover and cook for an additional 30 minutes, while stirring occasionally.

5 Move the Dutch oven further from the center of the fire and cook until the cabbage is extremely soft and browned, about 1 hour. Season with white pepper to taste.

6 About 20 minutes before the cabbage will be finished cooking, bring a pot of salted water to a boil. Place the egg noodles in the boiling water and cook until they are al dente, about 8 minutes. Drain, transfer to a large bowl, add the cabbage, and toss to combine. Serve immediately.

Polenta Cake with Greens

YIELD: 4 TO 6 SERVINGS • ACTIVE TIME: 30 MINUTES • TOTAL TIME: 1 HOUR

Polenta is cornmeal cooked into porridge and then baked or fried. It forms a lovely, bright yellow cake that is moist yet firm. It can be topped with all kinds of things, but in this recipe, it is the base for sautéed vegetables. Delicious!

INGREDIENTS

3 TABLESPOONS OLIVE OIL, PLUS MORE FOR DUTCH OVEN

1 CUP POLENTA

3 CUPS WATER

SALT AND PEPPER, TO TASTE

1 LB. BITTER GREENS (KALE, SWISS CHARD, ESCAROLE, OR DANDELION), STEMMED

3 GARLIC CLOVES, CHOPPED

RED PEPPER FLAKES, TO TASTE

ROMANO CHEESE, GRATED, FOR TOPPING

DIRECTIONS

1 Position a grate over the fire using gloved hands and tongs. Make sure the grate is as secure and level as possible.

2 Liberally oil a cast-iron Dutch oven and warm it for a few minutes.

3 In a heavy saucepan, whisk together the polenta and water. Bring to a boil, whisking to prevent lumps from forming. When bubbling, move the pan further from the center of the fire and simmer, uncovered, for a couple of minutes or until smooth. Season with salt and pepper.

4 Pour the polenta into the Dutch oven. Bake for about 30 minutes, turning the Dutch oven every few minutes to avoid burn spots, until the polenta is lightly golden and coming away from the edge of the pot.

5 While it's baking, make the greens. Bring a large pot of salted water to a boil, add the greens, and boil until very tender, 15 to 20 minutes. Drain in a colander and squeeze to remove excess moisture. Cut the greens into pieces. Heat the 3 tablespoons of olive oil in a pan, add the garlic, and cook, while stirring, until fragrant, about 2 minutes. Add the red pepper flakes, stir, and then add the greens. Cook until heated through. Season with salt and pepper. Keep warm until polenta is cooked.

6 Cut the polenta into wedges, top with greens, and sprinkle with Romano.

VARIATION: Substitute ½ lb. baby spinach leaves and ½ lb. kale (tough stems removed) for the 1 lb. of mixed greens.

Spicy Shrimp Polenta

YIELD: 4 TO 6 SERVINGS • ACTIVE TIME: 30 MINUTES • TOTAL TIME: 1 HOUR

If you're looking for a recipe for fun finger food, this is it—essentially a take on fish tacos but much easier to eat while standing. Plus, it's naturally gluten-free.

INGREDIENTS

3 TABLESPOONS CANOLA OIL

½ LB. SMALL SHRIMP, THAWED (IF FROZEN), PEELED, AND HALVED

1 CUP POLENTA

3 CUPS WATER

1 TEASPOON HORSERADISH, OR TO TASTE

1 TEASPOON RED PEPPER FLAKES

SALT AND PEPPER, TO TASTE

FRESH CILANTRO, FOR GARNISH

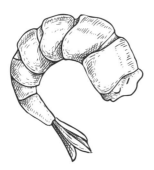

DIRECTIONS

1 Position a grate over the fire using gloved hands and tongs. Make sure the grate is as secure and level as possible.

2 When the coals are glowing, heat the canola oil in a Dutch oven. When hot but not smoking, add the shrimp. Stirring constantly and with a light touch, sauté the shrimp until just pink, about 3 to 5 minutes. Remove from heat and use a slotted spoon to transfer the shrimp to a paper towel–lined plate. Keep the oil in the Dutch oven.

3 In a heavy saucepan, whisk together the polenta and water. Bring to a boil, whisking to prevent lumps from forming. When bubbling, move the pan further from the center of the fire and simmer, uncovered, for a couple of minutes or until smooth. Remove the saucepan from heat and stir in the horseradish and red pepper flakes. Season with salt and pepper. Taste the polenta to see if the horseradish is strong enough for you. If you think it could use more, add another ½ teaspoon, but be careful not to overdo it. Stir in the shrimp.

4 Pour the polenta into the Dutch oven, smoothing the surface with the back of a spoon. Bake for about 30 minutes, turning the Dutch oven every few minutes to avoid burn spots. Bake until the polenta is lightly golden and coming away from the edge of the Dutch oven. Allow to cool for 5 to 10 minutes, then work quickly and carefully to invert the polenta cake onto a platter. Allow to cool to room temperature.

5 Cut the polenta into wedges and top each piece with a sprig of cilantro. Serve immediately.

Biscuits

YIELD: 4 TO 6 SERVINGS • ACTIVE TIME: 20 MINUTES • TOTAL TIME: 40 MINUTES

For fluffy buttermilk biscuits, you need to work with a very hot Dutch oven. The golden crust on the bottom is as much of a delight as the airy, warm dough.

INGREDIENTS

2 CUPS ALL-PURPOSE FLOUR, PLUS MORE FOR DUSTING

1 TEASPOON SUGAR

1 TEASPOON SALT

1 TABLESPOON BAKING POWDER

1 STICK OF UNSALTED BUTTER, CUT INTO PIECES

½ CUP BUTTERMILK, PLUS 2 TABLESPOONS

DIRECTIONS

1 Position a grate over the fire using gloved hands and tongs. Make sure the grate is as secure and level as possible.

2 In a large bowl, combine the flour, sugar, salt, and baking powder.

3 Using a fork or pastry knife, blend in 6 tablespoons of the butter to form a crumbly dough. Form a well in the middle and add ½ cup of the buttermilk. Stir to combine and form a stiff dough. Using your fingers works best. If it seems too dry, add 1 tablespoon more of the buttermilk, going to 2 tablespoons if necessary.

4 When the coals are glowing, put the remaining butter in a cast-iron Dutch oven.

5 Put the dough on a lightly floured surface and press out to a thickness of about 1 inch. Cut out biscuits using an inverted water glass. Place the biscuits in the Dutch oven and bake for about 10 minutes, turning the Dutch oven every few minutes to avoid burn spots. When the biscuits are golden on the bottom, remove from heat and serve.

VARIATIONS: Biscuits can be served with savory or sweet additions. You can make miniature ham sandwiches by splitting the biscuits, putting some mayonnaise and grainy mustard on them, and putting in a slice of fresh-baked ham. You can fill them with scrambled eggs and bacon bits. You can slather them with butter and your favorite jam or honey. Or just eat them as is.

Whole Wheat Cranberry & Pecan Bread

YIELD: 1 SMALL LOAF • ACTIVE TIME: 25 MINUTES • TOTAL TIME: 3 HOURS

This is a delicious, dense bread that is especially good toasted and served with fresh butter or cream cheese. It also makes a great complement to soft cheeses when cut into small pieces and served in place of crackers.

INGREDIENTS

¼ TEASPOON INSTANT YEAST

¼ TEASPOON SUGAR

1½ CUPS WATER (110 TO 115°F)

1 TEASPOON KOSHER SALT

2 CUPS WHOLE WHEAT FLOUR

1 CUP ALL-PURPOSE FLOUR, PLUS MORE FOR DUSTING

1 CUP DRIED CRANBERRIES

1 CUP PECANS, CHOPPED

DIRECTIONS

1 Put the yeast and sugar in a measuring cup and drizzle in about ½ cup warm water. Hot water will kill the yeast, so it's important that the water be warm without being hot. Cover the measuring cup with plastic wrap and set it aside for about 15 minutes. If the yeast doesn't foam, it is not alive and you'll need to start over.

2 When the yeast is proofed, pour it into a large bowl and add the remaining cup of warm water. Stir gently to combine. Combine the whole wheat flour and the all-purpose flour in a bowl. Add the salt to the flours, and then add the flour mixture to the yeast mixture. Stir with a wooden spoon until combined. The dough will be wet and sticky.

3 Put a dusting of all-purpose flour on a flat surface and lift out the dough. With flour on your hands and more at the ready, begin kneading the dough so that it loses its stickiness. As you're kneading, add in the cranberries and pecans so that they're distributed evenly in the dough. Don't overdo it, and don't use too much flour, just enough that the dough becomes more cohesive, about 5 minutes.

4 Place the dough in a large bowl, cover the bowl with plastic wrap, and allow to rise untouched until it has roughly doubled in size, at least 1 hour and up to several hours. Gently punch it down, score the top with a sharp knife, re-cover with the plastic, and allow to rise again for another 30 minutes or so.

Continued...

5 While the dough is on its final rise, position a grate over the fire using gloved hands and tongs. Make sure the grate is as secure and level as possible. Put a piece of parchment paper on the bottom of a cast-iron Dutch oven and put it on the grate with the lid on so it gets hot. When the coals are glowing and the dough has risen, carefully remove the lid and gently scoop the dough from the bowl into the pot, scored side up. Cover and bake for 15 minutes, turning every few minutes to avoid burn spots. Remove the lid and continue to bake for another 15 to 20 minutes, until the top is golden and it sounds hollow when tapped.

6 Remove the pot from the grate and use kitchen towels to carefully remove the bread. Allow to cool before slicing.

No-Knead Bread

YIELD: 1 SMALL LOAF • ACTIVE TIME: 20 MINUTES • TOTAL TIME: 24 HOURS

Use a 7-quart cast-iron Dutch oven for this recipe. This delicious bread is a great way to upgrade a pimento cheese sandwich—there is really nothing easier. Just remember that it takes up to two days to make, so plan ahead!

INGREDIENTS

½ TABLESPOON ACTIVE DRY YEAST

¼ TEASPOON SUGAR

1½ CUPS WATER (110 TO 115°F)

1½ TEASPOONS KOSHER SALT

3 CUPS ALL-PURPOSE FLOUR, PLUS MORE FOR DUSTING

DIRECTIONS

1 In a large bowl, add the yeast and sugar and top with the warm water. Stir to dissolve the yeast. Cover the measuring cup with plastic wrap and set it aside for about 15 minutes. If the yeast doesn't foam, it is not alive and you'll need to start over.

2 When the yeast is proofed, add the salt and flour. Stir until just blended with the yeast, sugar, and water. The dough will be sticky.

3 Cover the bowl with plastic wrap and set aside for at least 15 hours and up to 18 hours, preferably in a place that's 65 to 70°F.

4 The dough will be bubbly when you go to work with it. Lightly dust a work surface with flour and scoop the dough out onto it. Dust your fingers with flour so they don't stick to the dough. Fold it gently once or twice.

5 Transfer the dough to a clean, room-temperature bowl and cover with a kitchen towel. Let stand until doubled in size, another 1 to 2 hours.

6 While the dough is on its final rise, position a grate over the fire using gloved hands and tongs. Make sure the grate is as secure and level as possible. When the coals are glowing, place a cast-iron Dutch oven on the grate with the lid on so it gets hot. When the dough has risen, carefully remove the lid and gently scoop the dough from the bowl into the Dutch oven. Cover and bake for 20 minutes, turning the Dutch oven every few minutes to avoid burn spots. Remove the lid and continue to bake for another 25 minutes, until the top is golden and it sounds hollow when tapped.

Continued...

7 Remove the Dutch oven from the grate and use kitchen towels to carefully transfer bread to a rack or cutting board. Allow to cool at least 20 minutes before serving.

Simply Sensational Irish Soda Bread

YIELD: 1 LOAF • ACTIVE TIME: 30 MINUTES • TOTAL TIME: 1 HOUR AND 30 MINUTES

It wouldn't be St. Patrick's Day without Irish soda bread. According to the Culinary Institute of America, "With a history spanning more than two centuries, soda bread is a traditional Irish specialty. The first loaf, consisting of little more than flour, baking soda, salt, and sour milk, made its debut in the mid-1800s when baking soda found its way into Irish kitchens."

INGREDIENTS

4 CUPS ALL-PURPOSE FLOUR

½ CUP SUGAR

⅛ TEASPOON SALT

3¼ TEASPOONS BAKING POWDER

½ TEASPOON BAKING SODA

2 TABLESPOONS CARAWAY SEEDS

2 LARGE EGGS, LIGHTLY BEATEN

1½ CUPS BUTTERMILK

½ LB. RAISINS

UNSALTED BUTTER FOR THE DUTCH OVEN, PLUS MORE FOR SERVING

ORANGE MARMALADE, FOR SERVING

DIRECTIONS

1 Position a grate over the fire using gloved hands and tongs. Make sure the grate is as secure and level as possible.

2 Combine the flour, sugar, salt, baking powder, baking soda, and caraway seeds in a large mixing bowl. Add the beaten eggs and stir to combine. Gradually add the buttermilk until the dough is sticky and messy. Stir in the raisins.

3 Generously butter a cast-iron Dutch oven. Scoop and spread the dough in it.

4 When the coals are glowing, place the Dutch oven on the grate and bake for about 1 hour, turning the Dutch oven every few minutes to avoid burn spots. When done, the top should be crusty and brown and the bread sound hollow when tapped. Insert a toothpick in the center to be sure the dough is cooked through; the toothpick should come out clean.

5 Remove from heat, let cool slightly, and serve with fresh butter and orange marmalade.

Cheesy Soda Bread with Chives

YIELD: 1 LOAF • ACTIVE TIME: 40 MINUTES • TOTAL TIME: 1 HOUR AND 30 MINUTES

If you're looking for a savory version of a simple soda bread to serve with soup or stew, this is a great recipe.

INGREDIENTS

3 CUPS ALL-PURPOSE FLOUR

2 CUPS SPELT FLOUR

¾ CUP ROLLED OATS (NOT INSTANT)

2 TABLESPOONS SUGAR

1 TABLESPOON BAKING POWDER

1 TEASPOON SALT

1 TEASPOON BAKING SODA

1 STICK OF BUTTER, MELTED AND COOLED, PLUS MORE FOR THE DUTCH OVEN

2½ CUPS BUTTERMILK

1 LARGE EGG, LIGHTLY BEATEN

¼ CUP CHOPPED CHIVES

1¼ CUPS GRATED SHARP WHITE CHEDDAR CHEESE

FRESHLY GROUND BLACK PEPPER, TO TASTE

DIRECTIONS

1 Position a grate over the fire using gloved hands and tongs. Make sure the grate is as secure and level as possible.

2 In a large bowl, combine the flours, oats, sugar, baking powder, salt, and baking soda. Whisk to combine thoroughly. In another bowl, combine the butter, buttermilk, and egg.

3 Add the buttermilk mixture to the flour mixture and stir vigorously to blend. The dough will be sticky. Stir in the chives and 1 cup of the grated cheese.

4 Liberally grease a cast-iron Dutch oven with butter. Scoop and spread the dough into the Dutch oven. Sprinkle the black pepper over the top, then sprinkle the remaining cheese over it. Using a sharp knife, make an "x" in the center of the dough, about ½-inch deep, to settle the cheese farther into the dough as it cooks.

5 When the coals are glowing, bake for about 1 hour and 15 minutes, turning the Dutch oven every few minutes to avoid burn spots. When done, it should be golden on top and a toothpick inserted in the center will come out clean. Allow to sit in the Dutch oven for a few minutes before serving.

Olive Loaf

YIELD: 1 SMALL LOAF • ACTIVE TIME: 25 MINUTES • TOTAL TIME: 3 HOURS

The earthy-salty flavor of dark olives like Kalamatas is delicious in bread, too. If you don't want to take the time to slice a lot of Kalamata olives, use a top-shelf tapenade spread, which is easy to distribute in the dough.

INGREDIENTS

¼ TEASPOON INSTANT YEAST

¼ TEASPOON SUGAR

1½ CUPS WATER (110 TO 115°F)

1 TEASPOON KOSHER SALT

3 CUPS ALL-PURPOSE FLOUR, PLUS MORE FOR DUSTING

½ CUP TAPENADE OR KALAMATA OLIVES

1 TABLESPOON OLIVE OIL

DIRECTIONS

1 Put the yeast and sugar in a measuring cup and drizzle in about ½ cup warm water. Hot water will kill the yeast, so it's important that the water be warm without being hot. Cover the measuring cup with plastic wrap and set it aside for about 15 minutes. If the yeast doesn't foam, it is not alive and you'll need to start over.

2 When the yeast is proofed, pour it into a large bowl and add the remaining cup of warm water. Stir gently to combine. Add the salt to the flour and add the dry mixture to the yeast mixture. Stir with a wooden spoon until combined. The dough will be wet and sticky.

3 Put a dusting of flour on a flat surface and lift out the dough. With flour on your hands and more at the ready, begin kneading the dough so that it loses its stickiness. Don't overdo it, and don't use too much flour, just enough that it becomes more cohesive, about 5 minutes. Incorporate the tapenade or olive pieces while you're kneading.

4 Place the dough in a large bowl, cover the bowl with plastic wrap, and allow to rise untouched for at least 1 hour and up to several hours, until doubled in size. Gently punch it down, re-cover with the plastic, and allow to rise again for another 30 minutes or so. Brush with the olive oil.

Continued...

5 While the dough is on its final rise, position a grate over the fire using gloved hands and tongs. Make sure the grate is as secure and level as possible. Put a piece of parchment paper on the bottom of a cast-iron Dutch oven and put it on the grate with the lid on so it gets hot. When the coals are glowing and the dough has risen, carefully remove the lid and gently scoop the dough from the bowl into the pot. Cover and bake for 15 minutes, turning the Dutch oven every few minutes to avoid burn spots. Remove the lid and continue to bake for another 15 to 20 minutes, until the top is golden and it sounds hollow when tapped.

6 Remove the pot from heat and use kitchen towels or tongs to carefully remove the bread from the Dutch oven. Let the loaf cool completely before slicing.

Focaccia

YIELD: 4 TO 6 SERVINGS · ACTIVE TIME: 1 HOUR AND 30 MINUTES · TOTAL TIME: 3 HOURS

This is essentially a raised flatbread—like a crustier pizza—to which all kinds of yummy things can be added. It's become synonymous with Italian cuisine, and it's certainly popular in Italy, but it's also made throughout the Mediterranean region. You can find it in grocery stores, but there's nothing like a fresh piece right out of the Dutch oven, still warm, with the exact toppings you want. This one is simple, as it needs nothing more than salt and some Parmesan cheese.

INGREDIENTS

1 PACKET OF ACTIVE DRY YEAST (2¼ TEASPOONS)

2 CUPS WATER (110 TO 115°F)

4-4½ CUPS ALL-PURPOSE FLOUR, PLUS MORE FOR DUSTING

2 TEASPOONS SALT

2 TABLESPOONS OLIVE OIL, PLUS MORE FOR DRIZZLING

SEA SALT AND FRESHLY GROUND BLACK PEPPER, TO TASTE

PARMESAN CHEESE, GRATED, FOR TOPPING

DIRECTIONS

1 Proof the yeast by mixing it with the warm water. Let sit for 10 minutes until foamy.

2 In a bowl, combine the flour, salt, and yeast mix. Stir to combine. Transfer to a lightly floured surface and knead the dough until it loses its stickiness, adding more flour as needed, about 10 minutes.

3 Coat the bottom and sides of a large mixing bowl with a tablespoon of the olive oil. Place the ball of dough in the bowl, cover loosely with plastic wrap, put it in a naturally warm, draft-free location, and let it rise until doubled in size, about 45 minutes to 1 hour.

4 Position a grate over the fire using gloved hands and tongs. Make sure the grate is as secure and level as possible.

5 When doubled in size, turn the dough out onto a lightly floured surface and divide it in half. Put a tablespoon of the olive oil in a cast-iron Dutch oven, and press one of the pieces of dough into it. Drizzle some olive oil over it and sprinkle with salt and pepper, then with Parmesan. Cover loosely with plastic wrap and let rise for about 20 minutes. With the other piece, press it out onto a piece of parchment paper, follow the same procedure to top it, and let it rise.

Continued...

6 When the coals are glowing, put the Dutch oven on the grate and bake for 25 to 30 minutes, until golden brown. Turn the Dutch oven every few minutes to avoid burn spots. Remove from heat and let rest for 5 minutes before removing the focaccia from the Dutch oven to cool further. Wipe any crumbs out of the Dutch oven, coat with more olive oil, and transfer the other round to the Dutch oven. Bake for about 25 minutes, remove from Dutch oven, and let cool.

Caramelized Onion & Leek Focaccia

YIELD: 4 TO 6 SERVINGS • ACTIVE TIME: 2 HOURS • TOTAL TIME: 3 HOURS

Caramelized onions, when sautéed in butter and oil until soft and browned, lose their bite and are transformed into something almost sweet. The addition of leeks makes for a more subtle and slightly sweeter topping.

INGREDIENTS

1 STICK OF UNSALTED BUTTER

¼ CUP OLIVE OIL

1 YELLOW ONION, SLICED THIN

1 LARGE LEEK, WHITE AND LIGHT GREEN PARTS ONLY, SLICED THIN, AND RINSED WELL

1 TEASPOON ACTIVE DRY YEAST

1 CUP WATER (110 TO 115°F)

2-2½ CUPS ALL-PURPOSE FLOUR, PLUS MORE FOR DUSTING

1 TEASPOON KOSHER SALT

1 TEASPOON FRESHLY GROUND BLACK PEPPER, PLUS MORE FOR TOPPING

SEA SALT, FOR TOPPING

PARMESAN CHEESE, GRATED, FOR TOPPING

DIRECTIONS

1 Position a grate over the fire using gloved hands and tongs. Make sure the grate is as secure and level as possible.

2 When the coals are glowing, add the butter and 2 tablespoons of the oil in a cast-iron Dutch oven. When the butter is melted, add the onion and leek slices. Move the Dutch oven closer to the center of the fire and cook, while stirring, until the onion and leek start to soften, about 5 minutes. Move the Dutch oven further away from the center of the fire and allow to cook, stirring occasionally, until cooked down and browned, about 10 to 15 minutes. Set aside.

3 Proof the yeast by mixing it with the warm water. Let sit for 10 minutes until foamy.

4 Combine the flour, kosher salt, and pepper, and stir into the yeast mixture. Stir to combine well. The dough will be sticky. Transfer to a floured surface and knead the dough until it loses its stickiness, adding more flour as needed, about 10 minutes.

5 Coat the bottom and sides of a large mixing bowl with a tablespoon of the olive oil. Place the ball of dough in the bowl, cover loosely with plastic wrap, put it in a naturally warm, draft-free location, and let it rise until doubled in size, about 45 minutes to 1 hour.

Continued...

6 Put the remaining olive oil in the Dutch oven, and press the dough into it. Top with the caramelized onion/leek mix. Season generously with sea salt and pepper, then with Parmesan cheese. Cover loosely with plastic wrap and let rise for about 20 minutes.

7 Remove the plastic wrap and bake, turning the Dutch oven every few minutes to avoid burn spots, for 25 to 30 minutes, until golden brown. Remove from the grate and let rest for 5 minutes before removing from the Dutch oven to cool further.

Spinach & Ricotta Calzone

YIELD: 4 TO 6 SERVINGS • ACTIVE TIME: 1 HOUR • TOTAL TIME: 2 HOURS

This pizza "pie" is gooey with cheese and plenty of lovely green spinach. If you want to spice this up, try some red pepper flakes, either in the calzone or on the side.

INGREDIENTS

FOR THE FILLING

2 TABLESPOONS OLIVE OIL

3 GARLIC CLOVES, MINCED

1 TEASPOON RED PEPPER FLAKES (OPTIONAL)

1 LB. FROZEN CHOPPED SPINACH

SALT AND PEPPER, TO TASTE

2 CUPS FRESH RICOTTA CHEESE

1 EGG, LIGHTLY BEATEN

½ CUP GRATED PARMESAN CHEESE

FOR THE DOUGH

1½ CUPS WATER (110 TO 115°F)

2 TEASPOONS ACTIVE DRY YEAST

4 CUPS ALL-PURPOSE FLOUR, PLUS MORE FOR DUSTING

2 TEASPOONS SALT

DIRECTIONS

1 Position a grate over the fire using gloved hands and tongs. Make sure the grate is as secure and level as possible.

2 When the coals are glowing, place the olive oil, garlic, and red pepper flakes, if using, in a cast-iron Dutch oven. Add the frozen spinach. Cook, while stirring, until the spinach is completely thawed, about 5 minutes.

3 Move the Dutch oven further from the center of the fire and cover, stirring occasionally, until the spinach is cooked through, another 15 minutes. Season with salt and pepper. Set aside. In a bowl, mix together the ricotta, egg, and Parmesan cheese.

4 To make the dough, combine the warm water and yeast in a large bowl, stirring to dissolve the yeast. When the mixture starts to foam, stir in the flour and salt and mix until the dough is just combined. It will be sticky.

5 Turn the dough out on a floured surface and start kneading until the flour is incorporated, adding more if necessary to make the dough malleable and smooth but not overdone.

6 Lightly grease a bowl and put the dough in it. Allow to rise while you prepare the filling, about 30 minutes.

7 On a lightly floured surface, turn out the dough and separate it into two equal pieces. Roll each piece into a 12-inch circle.

Continued...

8 Place one circle in the Dutch oven. Spread the cooked spinach mixture evenly over the dough, then dollop with the ricotta mixture. Use a spatula or the back of a large spoon to distribute the ricotta mixture. Place the other dough circle over the filling and crimp to seal the edges together with your fingers. Cut 4 slits in the top.

9 Bake for 25 minutes, turning the Dutch oven every few minutes to avoid burn spots. When the crust is golden brown, remove from heat and allow to cool for about 10 minutes before slicing and serving.

Pepperoni Bread

YIELD: 6 TO 8 SERVINGS • ACTIVE TIME: 1 HOUR • TOTAL TIME: 3 HOURS

This is a good recipe for a lazy day at the campsite. Start in the morning for an afternoon bread, as the dough needs to rise several times.

INGREDIENTS

1½ TEASPOONS ACTIVE DRY YEAST

1¼ CUPS WATER (110 TO 115°F)

1 TABLESPOON SUGAR

1½ TEASPOONS SALT, PLUS MORE TO TASTE

3½ CUPS ALL-PURPOSE FLOUR, PLUS MORE FOR DUSTING

FRESHLY GROUND BLACK PEPPER, TO TASTE

½ LB. PEPPERONI, SLIVERED

2 CUPS GRATED MOZZARELLA CHEESE

1 TEASPOON RED PEPPER FLAKES

1 TEASPOON DRIED OREGANO

1 TEASPOON GARLIC POWDER

1 TABLESPOON UNSALTED BUTTER, MELTED

DIRECTIONS

1 Proof the yeast by mixing it with the water and sugar in a large bowl and then stirring. Let sit until foamy, about 10 minutes. Add the salt and about half the flour to form a sticky dough. Cover the bowl with plastic wrap or a clean kitchen towel and let rise in a warm, draft-free place until it has doubled in size, about 1 hour.

2 Punch down the dough and add the remaining flour. Transfer to a floured surface and knead the dough until it's smooth and elastic, 8 to 10 minutes. Transfer to a lightly greased bowl and let sit for about 15 minutes.

3 On the floured surface, roll the dough out into a rectangle about 14 x 16 inches. Sprinkle with salt and pepper, spread the pieces of pepperoni around the dough, then the cheese, and top with a sprinkling of hot pepper flakes, oregano, and garlic powder. Roll up so that the dough maintains its length and then slice the roll into 6 or 8 rounds.

4 Grease a cast-iron Dutch oven with the butter and place the rounds in it. Cover with a clean kitchen towel and let them rise for about 1 hour.

5 Position a grate over the fire using gloved hands and tongs. Make sure the grate is as secure and level as possible. Bake the pepperoni bread for about 30 minutes, turning the Dutch oven every few minutes to avoid burn spots. When the bread is golden on top and bubbling in the center, remove from heat and serve immediately.

VARIATION: It's easy to make this into a full-blown meat lover's bread. In addition to the pepperoni, add about ¼ to ½ cup of any or each of diced pancetta, diced smoked ham, crumbled cooked bacon, sautéed sausage, or diced cooked meatballs.

Pizza Dough

YIELD: 2 BALLS OF DOUGH • ACTIVE TIME: 30 MINUTES • TOTAL TIME: 1 HOUR

This is bread making at its simplest: flour, water, salt, and yeast. With this super-easy recipe, you can create amazing pizzas that can be personalized with almost anything you have, from traditional cheese to "gourmet." And while the flavor will become more complex and the crust crispier if you allow the dough to rise for a couple of hours, you can also roll it out and bake it within 15 minutes of making it.

INGREDIENTS

¾ CUP WATER (110 TO 115°F)

1 TEASPOON ACTIVE DRY YEAST

2 CUPS ALL-PURPOSE FLOUR, PLUS MORE FOR DUSTING

1½ TEASPOONS SALT

1 TABLESPOON OLIVE OIL

DIRECTIONS

1 If you'll be making pizza within the hour, position a grate over the fire using gloved hands and tongs. Make sure the grate is as secure and level as possible.

2 In a large bowl, add the warm water and yeast, stirring to dissolve the yeast. When the mixture starts to foam, stir in the flour and salt and mix until the dough is just combined. It will be sticky.

3 Turn out on a floured surface and start kneading until the flour is incorporated, adding more if necessary to make the dough malleable and smooth but not overdone.

4 If cooking immediately, allow the dough to rest for 15 minutes. While it's doing so, put a cast-iron Dutch oven on the grate to warm. Prepare the toppings for the pizza.

5 After 15 minutes, or when ready, put a piece of parchment paper under the dough. Start rolling and pushing it out to form a 9-inch round that will fit in the Dutch oven. If it bounces back, let it rest before pushing or rolling it out again.

6 When the round is formed, add the olive oil and brush to distribute over the bottom. Transfer the dough to the Dutch oven and add the toppings.

7 Bake for 12 to 15 minutes, turning the Dutch oven every few minutes to avoid burn spots. When the crust starts to brown and the toppings are hot and bubbling, remove and allow to cool for 5 minutes before lifting or sliding the pizza out and serving.

Classic Corn Bread

YIELD: 4 TO 6 SERVINGS • ACTIVE TIME: 1 HOUR • TOTAL TIME: 3 TO 4 HOURS

If you're going to make bread in cast iron, you have to make corn bread. In fact, many restaurants now serve corn bread right in a cast-iron pan.

INGREDIENTS

4 CUPS FINELY GROUND YELLOW CORNMEAL

¾ CUP SUGAR

1 TABLESPOON SALT

4 CUPS BOILING WATER

1 CUP ALL-PURPOSE FLOUR

1 TABLESPOON UNSALTED BUTTER, MELTED, PLUS 1 TEASPOON

2 EGGS, LIGHTLY BEATEN

2 TEASPOONS BAKING POWDER

1 TEASPOON BAKING SODA

1 CUP WHOLE MILK

DIRECTIONS

1 In a large bowl, combine the cornmeal, sugar, salt, and boiling water. Stir to combine and let sit for several hours in a cool, dark place. Stir occasionally while the batter is resting.

2 When ready to make, position a grate over the fire using gloved hands and tongs. Make sure the grate is as secure and level as possible.

3 Add flour, the 1 tablespoon of melted butter, eggs, baking powder, baking soda, and milk to the batter. Stir to thoroughly combine.

4 When the coals are glowing, heat a cast-iron Dutch oven and melt the teaspoon of butter in it. Add the batter.

5 Cook for 15 minutes, turning the Dutch oven every few minutes to avoid burn spots. Move the Dutch oven further from the center of the fire and cook for another 40 minutes, or until the bread is golden brown on top and set in the center.

Corn Tortillas

YIELD: 20 TORTILLAS • ACTIVE TIME: 50 MINUTES • TOTAL TIME: 50 MINUTES

You really should be making your own corn tortillas, as a warm tortilla lifted straight from a cast-iron griddle or skillet is a thing of beauty. The main ingredient, masa harina, is a corn flour that is available in most grocery stores.

INGREDIENTS

2 CUPS MASA HARINA, PLUS MORE AS NEEDED

½ TEASPOON SALT

1 CUP WARM WATER (110°F), PLUS MORE AS NEEDED

2 TABLESPOONS VEGETABLE OIL OR MELTED LARD

DIRECTIONS

1 Position a grate over the fire using gloved hands and tongs. Make sure the grate is as secure and level as possible.

2 Place the masa harina and salt in a bowl and stir to combine. Slowly add the warm water and oil (or lard) and stir until they are incorporated and a soft dough forms. The dough should be quite soft and not at all sticky. If it is too dry, add more water. If the dough is too wet, add more masa harina.

3 Wrap the dough in plastic (or place it in a resealable bag) and let it rest at room temperature for 30 minutes. It can be stored in a cooler for up to 24 hours; just be careful not to let it dry out.

4 Cut a 16-inch piece of plastic wrap and lay half of it across the bottom plate of a tortilla press.

5 When the coals are glowing, place a large cast-iron griddle on the grate over the center of the fire.

6 Pinch off a small piece of the dough and roll it into a ball. Place in the center of the lined tortilla press, fold the plastic over the top of the dough, and press down the top plate to flatten the dough. Do not use too much force. If the tortilla is too thin, you will have a hard time getting it off of the plastic. Open the press and carefully peel off the disk of dough. Reset the plastic.

7 Place the disk on the hot, dry griddle and toast for 30 to 45 seconds. Flip over and cook for another minute. Remove from the griddle and set aside. Repeat the process with the remaining dough.

Chickpea Crepes

YIELD: 6 CREPES • ACTIVE TIME: 10 MINUTES • TOTAL TIME: 10 MINUTES

These gluten-free crepes—known as besan pudla—are perfect as a side, but they can be so much more. Use them as you would a tortilla and wrap around grilled carrots, dal, and rice for an Indian twist on a taco. The first few may not come out perfectly, but don't let that deter you. It's all about working with the fire and getting a feel for the timing.

INGREDIENTS

2 CUPS CHICKPEA FLOUR

2 CUPS WATER

1 TEASPOON TURMERIC

½ TEASPOON SALT

3 GREEN ONIONS, SLICED THIN (OPTIONAL)

2 TABLESPOONS GHEE OR OLIVE OIL

DIRECTIONS

1 Position a grate over the fire using gloved hands and tongs. Make sure the grate is as secure and level as possible.

2 Place the chickpea flour, water, turmeric, salt, and green onions (if using) in a bowl and stir to combine. Let the mixture rest for 15 minutes.

3 When the coals are glowing, coat a cast-iron griddle lightly with some of the ghee or olive oil.

4 Pour ¼ cup of the batter onto the griddle and cook until bubbles appear evenly across the surface. Flip the crepe over and cook until it is firm. Transfer the cooked crepes to a plate and tent with tinfoil to keep warm. Repeat with the remaining batter, adding more ghee (or olive oil) if the griddle starts to look dry.

Pita Bread

YIELD: 16 PITAS • ACTIVE TIME: 1 HOUR • TOTAL TIME: 2 HOURS

Pitas are delicious, somewhat chewy bread pockets that originated in the Mediterranean region. They can be filled with just about anything and are popular around the world, but are especially prevalent in Middle Eastern cuisine.

INGREDIENTS

1 PACKET OF ACTIVE DRY YEAST (2¼ TEASPOONS)

2½ CUPS WARM WATER (110 TO 115°F)

3 CUPS ALL-PURPOSE FLOUR, PLUS MORE FOR DUSTING

1 TABLESPOON OLIVE OIL, PLUS MORE FOR THE SKILLET

1 TABLESPOON SALT

3 CUPS WHOLE WHEAT FLOUR

UNSALTED BUTTER, FOR GREASING THE BOWL

DIRECTIONS

1 Proof the yeast by mixing with the warm water. Let sit for about 10 minutes, until foamy.

2 In a large bowl, add the yeast mix into the all-purpose flour and stir until it forms a stiff dough. Cover and let the dough rise for about 1 hour.

3 Add the oil and salt to the dough and stir in the whole wheat flour in ½-cup increments. When finished, the dough should be soft. Turn onto a lightly floured surface and knead it until it is smooth and elastic, about 10 minutes.

4 Coat the bottom and sides of a large mixing bowl with butter. Place the ball of dough in the bowl, cover loosely with plastic wrap, put it in a naturally warm, draft-free location, and let it rise until doubled in size, about 45 minutes to 1 hour.

5 On a lightly floured surface, punch down the dough and cut into 16 pieces. Put the pieces on a baking sheet and cover with a kitchen towel while working with individual pieces.

6 Roll out the pieces with a rolling pin until they are approximately 7 inches across. Stack them between sheets of plastic wrap.

Continued...

7 Position a grate over the fire using gloved hands and tongs. Make sure the grate is as secure and level as possible. When the coals are glowing, warm a 10-inch cast-iron skillet over high heat and lightly oil the bottom. Cook the individual pitas for about 20 seconds on one side, then flip and cook for about a minute on the other side, until bubbles form. Turn again and continue to cook until the pita puffs up, another minute or so. Keep the skillet lightly oiled while cooking, and store the pitas on a plate under a clean kitchen towel until ready to serve.

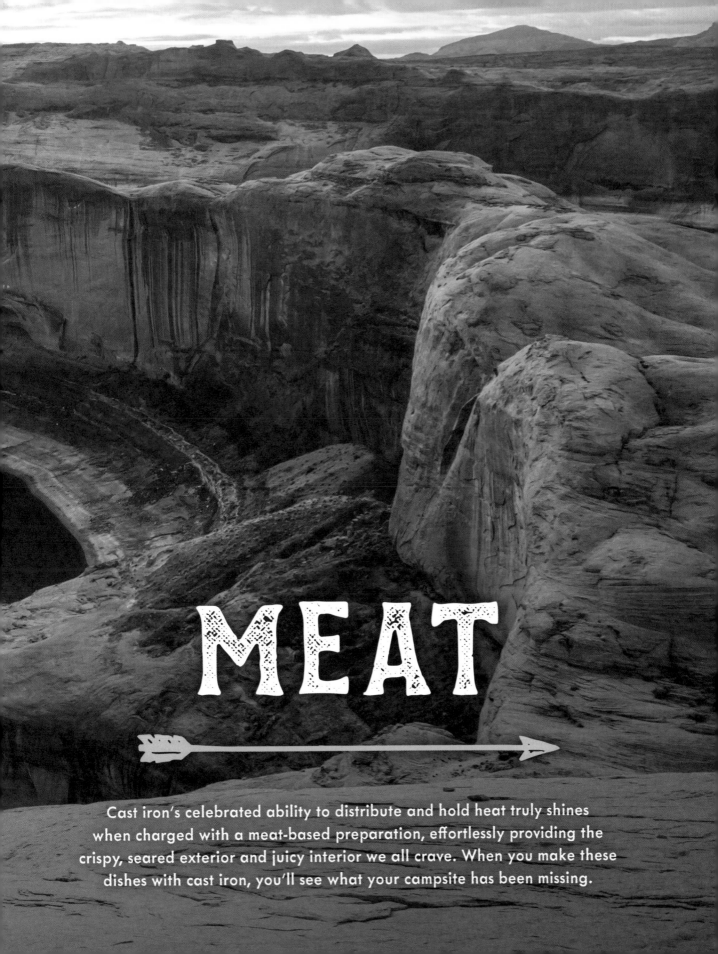

MEAT

Cast iron's celebrated ability to distribute and hold heat truly shines when charged with a meat-based preparation, effortlessly providing the crispy, seared exterior and juicy interior we all crave. When you make these dishes with cast iron, you'll see what your campsite has been missing.

Strip Steak with Mushrooms & Fingerling Potatoes

YIELD: 6 SERVINGS • ACTIVE TIME: 30 MINUTES • TOTAL TIME: 1 HOUR

For an added jolt of flavor, take whatever butter you have left over and mix it with some chopped thyme leaves. Place this on the steaks before serving and enjoy.

INGREDIENTS

2 TABLESPOONS KOSHER SALT OR COARSE SEA SALT

½ TEASPOON RED PEPPER FLAKES

½ TEASPOON WHOLE BLACK PEPPERCORNS

½ TEASPOON FENNEL SEEDS

½ TEASPOON MUSTARD SEEDS

½ TEASPOON CORIANDER SEEDS

6 (7 OZ.) STRIP STEAKS

2 LBS. FINGERLING POTATOES, HALVED LENGTHWISE

2 TABLESPOONS OLIVE OIL

1½ STICKS OF UNSALTED BUTTER, AT ROOM TEMPERATURE AND DIVIDED INTO 7 CHUNKS

6 SPRIGS OF THYME, PLUS 2 TABLESPOONS OF LEAVES FOR GARNISH

1 LARGE SHALLOT, MINCED

Continued...

DIRECTIONS

1 Position a grate over the fire using gloved hands and tongs. Make sure the grate is as secure and level as possible.

2 Place the salt and red pepper flakes in a bowl. Use a spice grinder or a mortar and pestle to grind the peppercorns, fennel seeds, mustard seeds, and coriander seeds into a powder. Place the powder in the bowl with the salt and red pepper flakes and stir to combine.

3 Place steaks on a plate and season liberally with the seasoning blend. Set the steaks aside and let stand at room temperature for 1 hour.

4 When the coals are glowing, place the potatoes in a 12-inch cast-iron skillet and cover with water. Cook until the potatoes are tender but not mushy. Drain and set aside.

5 Wipe the skillet with a paper towel, add the olive oil, and warm. Add the steaks to the skillet, making sure you don't overcrowd. Cook steaks for 2 minutes, turn them over, and add 1 chunk of butter and 1 sprig of thyme for each steak. Cook steaks for 2 minutes, while spooning the butter over the steaks. Remove steaks and set aside. Remove thyme sprigs and discard.

Continued...

2 LBS. CREMINI MUSHROOMS, CLEANED AND QUARTERED

1 LB. SHIITAKE MUSHROOMS, STEMMED AND SLICED THIN

1 LB. OYSTER MUSHROOMS, SLICED THIN

½ CUP CABERNET SAUVIGNON

¼ CUP WORCESTERSHIRE SAUCE

2 TABLESPOONS LIGHT TAMARI OR LIGHT SOY SAUCE

2 TABLESPOONS FISH SAUCE

6 Add the shallot and the remaining chunk of butter to the pan. Cook for 1 minute and add the cremini mushrooms. Cook for 5 minutes and then add the shiitake and oyster mushrooms. Cook for 3 more minutes and add the Cabernet Sauvignon. After 30 seconds, add the potatoes, Worcestershire sauce, tamari or soy sauce, and fish sauce. Stir until the mushrooms are evenly coated.

7 Return the steaks and their juices to the skillet. Cover the skillet and cook until the steaks are warmed through, about 3 minutes. If not done, check every few minutes until cooked to your liking.

8 Remove the skillet from heat and slice the steaks at a 45° angle every 2 inches. Scoop the potatoes and vegetables onto a plate, top with the sliced steak, sprinkle with the fresh thyme leaves, and serve.

Chicken with Herbs

YIELD: 4 SERVINGS • ACTIVE TIME: 10 MINUTES • TOTAL TIME: 40 MINUTES

When you want a dish that has lots of bright flavors but is still easy to make, this is the way to go. Serve it with mashed or roasted potatoes and a simply prepared vegetable, such as steamed green beans.

INGREDIENTS

1 TABLESPOON VEGETABLE OIL

1 LB. CHICKEN PIECES (BREASTS, LEGS, OR A COMBINATION)

1 SPRIG OF ROSEMARY

¼ CUP ALL-PURPOSE FLOUR

1 CUP CHICKEN BROTH

¼ CUP DRY WHITE WINE

2 TABLESPOONS DRIED OREGANO

2 TEASPOONS DRIED BASIL

2 TABLESPOONS UNSALTED BUTTER

1 TEASPOON DIJON MUSTARD

MASHED OR ROASTED POTATOES, FOR SERVING

SALT AND PEPPER, TO TASTE

STEAMED GREEN BEANS, FOR SERVING

DIRECTIONS

1 Position a grate over the fire using gloved hands and tongs. Make sure the grate is as secure and level as possible. Place a 10-inch cast-iron skillet on the grate to warm.

2 When the coals are glowing, add the oil, and then carefully place the chicken, skin side down, in the pan. Add the rosemary and cook for 15 minutes.

3 Use a spatula to turn the chicken over and cook for another 15 minutes.

4 Remove the chicken from the skillet and transfer to a platter.

5 Place the skillet over back on the grate, add the flour, and cook, while stirring, for 1 minute. Slowly whisk in the broth and wine and bring to a simmer. Add the dried oregano and basil and allow the mixture to simmer until it thickens slightly, about 5 minutes.

6 Add the butter and mustard, whisk to incorporate, and let the sauce simmer for another minute. Season with salt and pepper. Spoon the sauce over the chicken and serve with the potatoes and steamed green beans.

Steak au Poivre

YIELD: 2 SERVINGS • ACTIVE TIME: 40 MINUTES • TOTAL TIME: 2 HOURS

When making this French classic, keep in mind that you'll get the best results from the best ingredients. Go farm-fresh for the meat, shallots, chives, and cream, if at all possible. Bon appétit!

INGREDIENTS

2 (8 OZ.) BONELESS STRIP STEAKS

KOSHER SALT, TO TASTE

1 TABLESPOON WHOLE BLACK PEPPERCORNS

1 TEASPOON VEGETABLE OIL

2 TABLESPOONS UNSALTED BUTTER, CUT INTO PIECES

2 SMALL SHALLOTS, MINCED

⅓ CUP COGNAC OR OTHER BRANDY

½ CUP HEAVY CREAM

SPRIGS OF ROSEMARY, FOR GARNISH (OPTIONAL)

DIRECTIONS

1 Position a grate over the fire using gloved hands and tongs. Make sure the grate is as secure and level as possible.

2 Pat the steaks dry and season both sides with kosher salt.

3 Put the peppercorns in a sealed plastic bag and, working on a hard, flat surface, pound them with a meat tenderizer or mallet to crush them. Pour them onto a plate and press both sides of the steaks into them, distributing peppercorns evenly over the meat.

4 When the coals are glowing, place a 12-inch cast-iron skillet on the grate to heat for 5 minutes. Add the oil and swirl to coat the bottom of the pan. Put the steaks in the pan and sear on both sides, cooking for about 3 minutes a side for medium-rare.

5 Transfer steaks to a platter off to the side and keep warm as you make the sauce.

6 Add a tablespoon of the butter to the skillet, let it melt, and add the shallots. As they sauté, stir up the bits stuck to the bottom of the pan. Cook until shallots are browned, about 3 minutes. Remove from heat, pour the Cognac in the pan, swirl it around, and using a long-handled lighter, ignite it. The flame will subside in a minute or so. Return to the fire and cook the sauce until it is nearly boiling, while stirring constantly.

7 Add the cream and any juices from the platter the steaks are on. Move the skillet further away from the center of the fire and cook the sauce until somewhat reduced, about 5 minutes. Stir in the remaining tablespoon of butter.

8 Put the steaks on a plate and pour the sauce over them. Garnish with rosemary, if desired.

Country Fried Steaks & Gravy

YIELD: 2 SERVINGS • ACTIVE TIME: 40 MINUTES • TOTAL TIME: 2 HOURS

Try your hand at one of the most iconic Southern inventions—the Country Fried Steak! Be advised: high-quality ingredients will go a long way in this dish.

INGREDIENTS

2 (4 OZ.) ROUND STEAKS OR CUBE STEAKS

KOSHER SALT, TO TASTE

1 CUP ALL-PURPOSE FLOUR, PLUS 2 TABLESPOONS

½ TEASPOON FRESHLY GROUND BLACK PEPPER, PLUS MORE TO TASTE

1 CUP PEANUT, VEGETABLE, OR CANOLA OIL

2 TABLESPOONS UNSALTED BUTTER, CUT INTO PIECES

¾ CUP WHOLE MILK, PLUS MORE AS NEEDED

DIRECTIONS

1 Position a grate over the fire using gloved hands and tongs. Make sure the grate is as secure and level as possible.

2 Prep steaks by patting them dry then seasoning both sides with kosher salt.

3 Add the cup of flour and ½ teaspoon of pepper to a shallow dish or bowl and dredge the steaks in it. Make sure they are evenly coated.

4 When the coals are glowing, place a 12-inch cast-iron skillet over the fire to warm for 5 minutes. Add the oil and the butter, coating the bottom of the pan. Put the steaks in the pan and fry on both sides, cooking for about 5 minutes a side.

5 Transfer steaks to a serving dish on the side of the grate and keep warm as you make the gravy.

6 For the gravy, move the skillet further from the center of the fire and pour out all but 2 tablespoons of the leftover pan drippings. Mix in the 2 tablespoons of flour, creating a roux. Continue to stir and move the skillet closer to the center of the fire.

7 Once the roux is smooth, slowly add the milk, stirring constantly until incorporated. If the gravy is too thick, add more milk. If too thin, continue to cook it until it reduces. Season with a sprinkle of salt and plenty of black pepper. Cover the steaks with the gravy and serve.

Buffalo Chicken Wings

YIELD: 4 SERVINGS • ACTIVE TIME: 30 MINUTES • TOTAL TIME: 45 MINUTES

This recipe can easily be altered, so don't hesitate to tinker.

INGREDIENTS

4 TABLESPOONS UNSALTED BUTTER

1 TABLESPOON WHITE VINEGAR

¾ CUP HOT SAUCE (TABASCO™ OR FRANK'S REDHOT® RECOMMENDED)

1 TEASPOON CAYENNE PEPPER (OPTIONAL)

6 CUPS VEGETABLE OIL

2 LBS. CHICKEN WINGS

1 CUP CORNSTARCH

SALT, TO TASTE

BLUE CHEESE DRESSING (SEE RECIPE), FOR SERVING

CELERY STICKS, FOR SERVING

BLUE CHEESE DRESSING

¼ CUP SOUR CREAM

¼ CUP MAYONNAISE

¼ CUP BUTTERMILK

1 TABLESPOON FRESH LEMON JUICE

PINCH OF BLACK PEPPER

1 CUP CRUMBLED BLUE CHEESE

DIRECTIONS

1 Position a grate over the fire using gloved hands and tongs. Make sure the grate is as secure and level as possible.

2 When the coals are glowing, place the butter in a large saucepan. When it has melted, whisk in the vinegar, hot sauce, and cayenne (if using), making sure not to breathe in the spicy steam. Remove the pan from heat and cover to keep warm while you cook the wings.

3 Place the vegetable oil in a large cast-iron Dutch oven and heat until hot. This can take up to 10 minutes.

4 While the oil is heating, pat the wings dry and, working in batches, toss them in the cornstarch.

5 Add the coated wings to the oil in batches and fry until they are crispy, about 10 minutes. Transfer the fried chicken wings to a wire rack and season with salt.

6 Add the cooked wings to the spicy sauce in the saucepan. Remove them with a slotted spoon, arrange them on a platter, and serve them with the Blue Cheese Dressing and celery sticks.

BLUE CHEESE DRESSING

1 Place the sour cream, mayonnaise, buttermilk, lemon juice, and pepper in a bowl and whisk to combine.

2 Add the blue cheese and stir to incorporate.

Classic Burgers

YIELD: 3 TO 4 BURGERS • ACTIVE TIME: 30 MINUTES • TOTAL TIME: 30 MINUTES

A burger hot off the grill is a delicious thing. It's a staple of American dining. But if you want the best burger ever, you won't produce it on the grill. You'll make it in a cast-iron skillet. Why? Because the fat in the meat creates its own sauce, helping to brown and flavor the meat as it cooks. All of this drips off the grill. The cast iron holds the heat steady and hot, too, turning the surface of the burger the perfect, crispy dark brown from side to side. If your mouth is watering now, wait until you make these at the campsite.

INGREDIENTS

1 LB. GROUND BEEF

VEGETABLE OIL, FOR THE SKILLET

SALT AND PEPPER, TO TASTE

HAMBURGER BUNS, FOR SERVING

SLICES OF CHEESE (OPTIONAL), FOR SERVING

LETTUCE, TOMATO, ONION (OPTIONAL), FOR SERVING

KETCHUP, MUSTARD, PICKLES, MAYONNAISE (OPTIONAL), FOR SERVING

DIRECTIONS

1 Keep the ground beef cool until ready to use. Position a grate over the fire using gloved hands and tongs. Make sure the grate is as secure and level as possible.

2 When it's time to make the burgers, brush a 12-inch cast-iron skillet with a thin sheen of oil. Don't overhandle the meat, simply take a handful of it (about 3 oz.) and form into a patty. Make 3 or 4, depending on how many will fit in the skillet.

3 Put the patties in the skillet and don't touch them. Let them start to cook. Sprinkle some salt and pepper over them. Let them cook on one side for about 3 minutes.

4 When you flip the burgers, if you want cheese on one or all of them, put it on now.

5 Leave the burgers to cook on this side for 3 or 4 minutes. Scoop the burgers off the skillet with the spatula, slide each one onto a bun, top with whatever you like, and enjoy.

TIP: The kind of meat you use matters. The meat-to-fat ratio should be about 80–20. Most ground beef found in the grocery store is 85–15 or 90–10. If you have to go with one of these, choose the fattier proportion. The best thing to do, though, is ask the meat department to grind the meat for you. You want a chuck cut with a good amount of fat in it. The fat should show up as almost chunky in the meat, not pulverized.

Lemon & Rosemary Chicken with Roasted Vegetables

YIELD: 4 SERVINGS • ACTIVE TIME: 25 MINUTES • TOTAL TIME: 1 HOUR

This classic recipe is perfect for any season. The sunny flavors of the lemon and rosemary mingle beautifully with the hearty roasted vegetables.

INGREDIENTS

2 EGGPLANTS, CHOPPED

3 BELL PEPPERS, STEMMED, SEEDS AND RIBS REMOVED, AND SLICED

2 ZUCCHINI, SLICED

2 CUPS CHERRY TOMATOES

1 ONION, CHOPPED

3 GARLIC CLOVES, MINCED

¼ CUP OLIVE OIL

SALT AND PEPPER, TO TASTE

4 BONELESS, SKINLESS CHICKEN BREASTS

2 TABLESPOONS FRESH LEMON JUICE

4 SPRIGS FRESH ROSEMARY

DIRECTIONS

1 Position a grate over the fire using gloved hands and tongs. Make sure the grate is as secure and level as possible.

2 When the coals are glowing, place all of the vegetables in a cast-iron Dutch oven, drizzle 2 tablespoons of the olive oil over the top, and season them with salt and pepper. Cover and roast until the zucchini is just tender, about 30 minutes, uncovering halfway through. Remove from heat and set aside.

3 While the vegetables are roasting, place the chicken breasts in a mixing bowl, season them with salt and pepper, and add the lemon juice. Toss until the chicken is coated and let them rest at room temperature.

4 Warm the remaining olive oil in a 12-inch cast-iron skillet. When the oil starts to shimmer, add the chicken breasts and cook until browned, about 4 minutes. Turn the chicken breasts over, add the rosemary to the pan, and begin basting the chicken breasts with the oil. Cook until browned on the other side, remove the pan from the grate, and continue to baste the chicken with the rosemary-infused oil.

5 Place the chicken breasts on the vegetables, drizzle any remaining infused oil over them, and cover the Dutch oven. Bake until the chicken breasts are cooked through, about 10 minutes. If not done, check every 5 minutes until cooked to your liking. Let them rest briefly before serving.

Beef Stroganoff

YIELD: 4 TO 6 SERVINGS • ACTIVE TIME: 40 MINUTES • TOTAL TIME: 1 HOUR AND 30 MINUTES

This dish is originally Russian and is made with pieces of beef served in a rich sauce that includes sour cream (smetana). It reportedly became popular in the mid-1800s. This is amazing on a cold winter day paired with a side of whole wheat bread and a cold cider.

INGREDIENTS

1 TABLESPOON OLIVE OIL, PLUS MORE AS NEEDED

1 LB. STEW BEEF, CUT INTO STRIPS

1 SMALL ONION, MINCED

2 GARLIC CLOVES, PRESSED

½ CUP SLICED MUSHROOM CAPS

1½ CUPS BEEF BROTH

¼ CUP DRY SHERRY

1 TABLESPOON WORCESTERSHIRE SAUCE

¼ CUP ALL-PURPOSE FLOUR

½ CUP SOUR CREAM

SALT AND PEPPER, TO TASTE

½ LB. EGG NOODLES, COOKED, FOR SERVING

DIRECTIONS

1 Position a grate over the fire using gloved hands and tongs. Make sure the grate is as secure and level as possible.

2 When the coals are glowing, heat the olive oil in a 12-inch cast-iron skillet. Add the beef strips so they fit in the skillet (or work in batches). Fry them in the skillet, while turning so that all sides get browned, about 3 minutes. Transfer the beef pieces to a plate and cover with foil to keep warm.

3 Add a bit more oil if necessary, and sauté the onion, garlic, and mushrooms until soft, about 5 minutes. In the skillet, add the beef broth, Sherry, and Worcestershire sauce. Bring to a boil, scraping the browned bits of meat and vegetables off the bottom of the pan. Put the flour in a bowl and add some of the heated sauce, using a whisk to form a paste. Add a bit more sauce to the bowl, and when the flour is fully incorporated, transfer all of it into the skillet and stir until incorporated. Continue to cook until the sauce thickens.

4 Move the skillet further from the center of the fire and add the sour cream. Add the beef back to the skillet. When everything is hot, season with salt and pepper, and serve over the egg noodles.

Chicken Bake

YIELD: 6 SERVINGS • ACTIVE TIME: 15 MINUTES • TOTAL TIME: 45 MINUTES

The tender, juicy chicken sucks up all of the delicious flavors in this dish. All of the flavors come together to create perfection.

INGREDIENTS

2 LBS. BONE-IN, SKIN-ON CHICKEN BREASTS, HALVED ALONG THEIR EQUATORS

SALT AND PEPPER, TO TASTE

1 TABLESPOON FINELY CHOPPED FRESH OREGANO

1 TEASPOON FINELY CHOPPED FRESH THYME

1 TEASPOON PAPRIKA

4 GARLIC CLOVES, MINCED

3 TABLESPOONS OLIVE OIL, PLUS MORE AS NEEDED

JUICE OF ½ LEMON

1 RED ONION, SLICED THIN

1 LB. TOMATOES, SLICED

FRESH BASIL LEAVES, FOR GARNISH

FRESH PARSLEY, FINELY CHOPPED, FOR GARNISH

DIRECTIONS

1 Position a grate over the fire using gloved hands and tongs. Make sure the grate is as secure and level as possible.

2 Place the chicken breasts in a bowl, season with salt and pepper, and then add the oregano, thyme, paprika, garlic, olive oil, and lemon juice. Stir until the chicken is evenly coated and set it aside.

3 Coat the bottom of a cast-iron Dutch oven with olive oil and then distribute the red onion over it. Place the chicken breasts on top, arrange the tomato slices on top, and cover the Dutch oven.

4 Roast for 10 minutes. Remove the lid and cook for another 5 to 7 minutes, until the chicken is cooked through. Remove from heat and let rest for 10 minutes before garnishing with the basil and parsley.

Thai Crying Tiger Beef

YIELD: 4 SERVINGS • ACTIVE TIME: 15 MINUTES • TOTAL TIME: 30 MINUTES

A lot of theories abound as to why this dish is called Crying (or Weeping) Tiger, but all of them agree that it is delicious. You may also end up with tears in your eyes, overwhelmed by the good fortune of happening upon this dish.

INGREDIENTS

2 LBS. FLANK STEAK

2 TABLESPOONS SOY SAUCE

1 TABLESPOON OYSTER SAUCE

1 TABLESPOON BROWN SUGAR, PLUS 1 TEASPOON

1 LARGE TOMATO, SEEDED AND DICED

⅓ CUP LIME JUICE

¼ CUP FISH SAUCE (OPTIONAL)

2 TABLESPOONS MINCED CILANTRO LEAVES

1½ TABLESPOONS TOASTED RICE POWDER (SEE RECIPE)

1 TABLESPOON RED PEPPER FLAKES

1 CUP SOFT HERB LEAF MIX (MINT, THAI HOLY BASIL, AND CILANTRO), FOR GARNISH

1½ CUPS COOKED WHITE RICE, FOR SERVING

TOASTED RICE POWDER

½ CUP JASMINE RICE

DIRECTIONS

1 Position a grate over the fire using gloved hands and tongs. Make sure the grate is as secure and level as possible.

2 Pat the steak dry. Place it in a bowl and add the soy sauce, oyster sauce, and the 1 tablespoon of brown sugar. Stir to combine and then let the steak marinate for 10 minutes.

3 When the coals are glowing, place a cast-iron grill pan over the grate and spray it with nonstick cooking spray. Add the steak and cook on each side for 5 minutes for medium. Transfer to a plate, cover with foil, and let rest for 5 minutes before slicing into thin strips, making sure to cut across the grain.

4 To make the dipping sauce, place the tomato, lime juice, fish sauce (if using), remaining brown sugar, cilantro, Toasted Rice Powder, and red pepper flakes in a bowl and stir to combine. The powder won't dissolve, but it will lightly bind the rest of the ingredients together.

5 Divide the dipping sauce between the serving bowls. Top with the slices of beef, garnish with the soft herb leaf mix, and serve alongside the white rice.

TOASTED RICE POWDER

1 Heat a cast-iron skillet. Add the rice and toast until browned.

2 Remove and grind into a fine powder with a mortar and pestle.

Pesto Chicken with Charred Tomatoes

YIELD: 4 SERVINGS • ACTIVE TIME: 5 MINUTES • TOTAL TIME: 3 HOURS

The pesto pairs beautifully with the tomatoes and packs on the flavor to simple chicken.

INGREDIENTS

2 LBS. CHICKEN PIECES

SALT AND PEPPER, TO TASTE

BASIL PESTO, TO TASTE

4 PLUM TOMATOES, HALVED

DIRECTIONS

1 Position a grate over the fire using gloved hands and tongs. Make sure the grate is as secure and level as possible.

2 Season the chicken with salt and pepper. Place the pesto in a bowl, add the chicken pieces, and stir until they are evenly coated. Cover the bowl and let the chicken marinate in the cooler for 2 hours.

3 Remove the chicken from the cooler and let it come to room temperature.

4 When the coals are glowing, place the chicken in a cast-iron Dutch oven. Season the tomatoes with salt and pepper and place them in the Dutch oven. Cover and roast for 25 minutes. Remove the lid and continue roasting until the chicken is cooked through, about 25 minutes. If not done, check every 5 to 10 minutes until cooked to your liking. Let the chicken rest for 10 minutes before serving.

Brazilian Pot Roast

YIELD: 4 TO 6 SERVINGS • ACTIVE TIME: 30 MINUTES • TOTAL TIME: 2 HOURS AND 30 MINUTES

This hearty and warming stew hails from northern Brazil. It's seasoned with annatto, a popular ingredient that is used to flavor and color meat. If you can't find annatto, you can either omit it or use turmeric, which will lend the dish a different deliciousness. If you want to be extra authentic, stir in 12 to 16 whole pods of okra for the last 15 minutes of cooking and serve with rice and black beans.

INGREDIENTS

4-LB. CHUCK ROAST

SALT AND PEPPER, TO TASTE

1 TABLESPOON ANNATTO POWDER (OPTIONAL)

1 TABLESPOON GROUND CUMIN

2 TABLESPOONS VEGETABLE OIL

2 LARGE CARROTS, PEELED AND CHOPPED

1 LARGE YELLOW ONION, CHOPPED

2 LARGE POTATOES, PEELED AND CHOPPED

5 GARLIC CLOVES, MINCED

2 CUPS BEEF BROTH

DIRECTIONS

1 Position a grate over the fire using gloved hands and tongs. Make sure the grate is as secure and level as possible.

2 Pat the chuck roast dry and season it lightly all over with salt, annatto (if using), and cumin.

3 When the coals are glowing, warm the vegetable oil in a large cast-iron Dutch oven. When the oil starts to smoke, add the chuck roast and cook until it is brown on all sides, 10 to 15 minutes, and more if needed. Remove the roast and set it aside.

4 Add the carrots, onion, potatoes, and garlic and cook until they are lightly browned, about 10 minutes. Return the roast to the Dutch oven and add the broth. It should not cover the meat.

5 Cover the Dutch oven. Cook until the roast is tender, about 2 hours, turning the Dutch oven every few minutes to prevent burn spots. Remove the roast from the pot, let it cool slightly, and then cut it into bite-sized pieces. Place the pieces back in the pot, stir to incorporate, and then ladle into warmed bowls.

Fried Chicken

YIELD: 4 SERVINGS • ACTIVE TIME: 1 HOUR • TOTAL TIME: 1 HOUR AND 30 MINUTES

If you want the texture and flavor of deep-fried chicken without the mess, try this recipe. The cornflakes are essential!

INGREDIENTS

3 CHICKEN LEGS, SEPARATED INTO DRUMSTICKS AND THIGHS

¼ CUP ALL-PURPOSE FLOUR

SALT AND PEPPER, TO TASTE

1 CUP WHOLE MILK

1 TABLESPOON WHITE VINEGAR

2 EGGS, LIGHTLY BEATEN

1½ CUPS CORNFLAKES, FINELY CRUSHED

½ CUP PLAIN BREAD CRUMBS

1 TEASPOON PAPRIKA

1 CUP VEGETABLE OIL

DIRECTIONS

1 Position a grate over the fire using gloved hands and tongs. Make sure the grate is as secure and level as possible. Place a cast-iron Dutch oven on the grate to get it hot.

2 Rinse and dry the chicken pieces.

3 In a shallow bowl or cake pan, whisk together the flour with some salt and pepper. Combine the milk and the vinegar and let the combination sit for 10 minutes to create buttermilk. When ready, place the buttermilk in a bowl with the beaten eggs. In another large bowl, combine the cornflakes, bread crumbs, paprika, and 2 tablespoons of the vegetable oil.

4 Coat the chicken pieces one at a time by dipping each in the flour, then the buttermilk mixture, then the crumb mixture, being sure to coat all sides. When coated, put the pieces on a plate, cover with plastic wrap, and put in a cooler for about 15 minutes.

5 When the coals are glowing, move the Dutch oven to the edge of the grate and warm the remaining oil in the Dutch oven until hot. Add the cold chicken pieces and turn in the hot oil until both sides are coated.

6 Cover and bake for about 30 minutes, turning the pieces after 15 minutes and turning the Dutch oven every few minutes to avoid burn spots. The chicken is done when the juices run clear when pierced with a knife. Serve immediately.

Hungarian Goulash

YIELD: 6 TO 8 SERVINGS • ACTIVE TIME: 30 MINUTES • TOTAL TIME: 2 HOURS AND 30 MINUTES

A rich and hearty dish that will be even better the next day. Redolent with the flavors of Eastern Europe—sweet paprika, earthy caraway, garlic, and sour cream—it is the comfort food you never knew you needed. Take your time making this; you will be rewarded.

INGREDIENTS

2 TABLESPOONS VEGETABLE OIL

3 LBS. BEEF CHUCK, TRIMMED

3 YELLOW ONIONS, CHOPPED

2 CARROTS, PEELED AND CHOPPED

2 BELL PEPPERS, SEEDED AND CHOPPED

1 TEASPOON CARAWAY SEEDS

¼ CUP ALL-PURPOSE FLOUR

3 TABLESPOONS SWEET HUNGARIAN PAPRIKA

3 TABLESPOONS TOMATO PASTE

2 GARLIC CLOVES, MINCED

1 TEASPOON SUGAR

SALT AND PEPPER, TO TASTE

2 CUPS BEEF BROTH

1 LB. WIDE EGG NOODLES

1 CUP SOUR CREAM

DIRECTIONS

1 Position a grate over the fire using gloved hands and tongs. Make sure the grate is as secure and level as possible.

2 When the coals are glowing, warm the oil in a large cast-iron Dutch oven. When the oil starts to smoke, add the meat in batches and cook until it is browned all over, taking care not to crowd the pot. Remove the browned meat and set aside.

3 Move the Dutch oven further away from the center of the fire. Wait 2 minutes to let cool slightly and then add the onions, carrots, and peppers. Stir to coat with the pan drippings and sauté until the vegetables are golden brown, about 10 minutes. Add the caraway seeds, stir to incorporate, and cook until the seeds are fragrant, about 1 minute.

4 Add the flour, paprika, tomato paste, garlic, sugar, salt, and pepper and stir to incorporate. Add the broth and use a wooden spoon to scrape up any browned bits from the bottom of the pot.

5 Bring the goulash to a boil, move the Dutch oven to the edge of the fire, and let it simmer until it thickens slightly, about 10 minutes. Add the meat back to the Dutch oven, cover, and simmer until the meat is very tender, about 2 hours. Turn the Dutch oven every few minutes to avoid burn spots.

6 Approximately 20 minutes before the goulash will be done, bring water to a boil in a large pot. Add the egg noodles to the boiling water and cook until al dente. Drain and set aside.

7 To serve, stir in the sour cream and ladle the goulash over the cooked egg noodles.

Rice & Beans with Chicken Thighs

YIELD: 6 SERVINGS • ACTIVE TIME: 15 MINUTES • TOTAL TIME: 1 HOUR AND 45 MINUTES

The cast-iron Dutch oven is a truly amazing piece of cooking equipment that allows you to cook this recipe nice and slow to really bring out the delicate flavors of the spices and create a dish that is second to none.

INGREDIENTS

½ LB. KIDNEY BEANS, SOAKED OVERNIGHT AND DRAINED

½ CUP VEGETABLE OIL

4 BONELESS, SKINLESS CHICKEN THIGHS

2 PIECES OF SALT PORK, MINCED (ABOUT ½ CUP)

1 CUP SOFRITO

1 CUP OF SPANISH-STYLE TOMATO SAUCE, PUREED

2 CUPS WHITE RICE

3 CUPS CHICKEN STOCK

2 PACKETS OF SAZÓN WITH ACHIOTE

2 TABLESPOONS DRIED OREGANO

1 CUP SPANISH OLIVES, WITH THE BRINE

ADOBO SEASONING, TO TASTE

DIRECTIONS

1 Position a grate over the fire using gloved hands and tongs. Make sure the grate is as secure and level as possible. If using a tripod, set up prior to building your fire. You will need a round bottomed cauldron or a Dutch oven with a hanging loop handle.

2 When the coals are glowing, place the beans in a cast-iron Dutch oven or a hanging cast-iron Dutch oven and cover with water. Bring to a boil, move the Dutch oven further from the center of the fire, and cover the pot. Cook for 45 minutes to 1 hour, until the beans are tender, turning the Dutch oven every few minutes to avoid burn spots. Drain and set the beans aside.

3 Place the pot back over the fire and add ¼ cup of the oil. Add the chicken and cook for about 5 minutes on each side. Remove the chicken from the Dutch oven, cut it into 12 pieces, and set aside.

4 Add the salt pork and the remaining oil to the pot and cook until some of the salt pork's fat has rendered, about 5 minutes. Add the sofrito and the tomato sauce. Cook for 5 minutes, stirring constantly.

5 Add the rice to the pot, stir, and cook for 5 minutes. Add the remaining ingredients and return the chicken to the pot. Move the Dutch oven further from the center of the fire and cook for 10 minutes. Cover the Dutch oven and cook for another 20 to 30 minutes, or until the liquid has been absorbed and the rice is tender.

Continued...

6 Uncover the pot and add the beans. Stir to combine and serve.

TIP: The rice at the bottom of the Dutch oven might get a little crunchy. That is actually preferred for this dish.

Shepherd's Pie

YIELD: 4 TO 6 SERVINGS • ACTIVE TIME: 45 MINUTES • TOTAL TIME: 1 HOUR AND 30 MINUTES

This "pie" doesn't have a crust. Instead, it has a top layer of mashed potatoes, which blankets the beef mixture and helps keep it juicy. In that sense, it works like a pie. Semantics aside, it's one of the best comfort foods you can make.

INGREDIENTS

6 RUSSET POTATOES, PEELED AND CUBED

½ TEASPOON SALT, PLUS MORE TO TASTE

1 STICK OF BUTTER, DIVIDED INTO TABLESPOONS

½ CUP WHOLE MILK

PLAIN YOGURT, AS NEEDED

FRESHLY GROUND BLACK PEPPER, TO TASTE

1 TABLESPOON OLIVE OIL

½ YELLOW ONION, MINCED

1 LB. GROUND BEEF

1 (14 OZ.) CAN OF PETIT POIS (PEAS), DRAINED, OR 2 CUPS HIGH-QUALITY FROZEN PEAS

½ (14 OZ.) CAN OF CORN, DRAINED (OPTIONAL)

DIRECTIONS

1 Position a grate over the fire using gloved hands and tongs. Make sure the grate is as secure and level as possible.

2 When the coals are glowing, put the potato pieces in a large saucepan or pot and cover with cold water. Add the salt. Bring the water to a boil, move the pot to the edge of the fire to bring to a simmer, and cook the potatoes until soft, about 20 minutes. When they can be easily pierced with a sharp knife, they're cooked.

3 Drain the potato pieces and put them in a large bowl. Add 6 tablespoons of the butter and the milk and use a potato masher to make the mashed potatoes. If the mashed potatoes are too soupy, add yogurt in 1-tablespoon increments until they are creamy. Season with salt and pepper and set aside.

4 Warm a cast-iron Dutch oven, add the olive oil and onion, and cook until the onion is just soft, about 2 minutes. Add the ground beef and stir to break apart while it browns. When there is just a little pink left in the meat, drain the fat from the Dutch oven. Stir in the peas and, if desired, the corn. Season with salt and pepper.

5 Spread the mashed potatoes over the meat and vegetables, distributing the potatoes evenly and smoothing the top. Cut the remaining 2 tablespoons of butter into slivers and dot the potatoes with them.

6 Cover and bake for 30 minutes, turning every few minutes to avoid burn spots. Remove the lid and cook for another 10 minutes until the potatoes are just browned. If not done, check every 15 minutes until cooked to your liking.

7 Allow to cool for 5 minutes before serving.

Chicken Kebabs

YIELD: 4 TO 6 SERVINGS • ACTIVE TIME: 20 MINUTES • TOTAL TIME: 2½ TO 24 HOURS

Once again, cast iron takes on a preparation that is universally associated with the grill and shows that it is more deserving of the job.

INGREDIENTS

2 TABLESPOONS PAPRIKA

1 TEASPOON TURMERIC

1 TEASPOON ONION POWDER

1 TEASPOON GARLIC POWDER

1 TABLESPOON DRIED OREGANO

¼ CUP OLIVE OIL, PLUS MORE AS NEEDED

2 TABLESPOONS WHITE WINE VINEGAR

1 CUP PLAIN GREEK YOGURT

1 TEASPOON KOSHER SALT, PLUS MORE TO TASTE

3 LBS. BONELESS, SKINLESS CHICKEN THIGHS, CUT INTO BITE-SIZED PIECES

FRESHLY GROUND BLACK PEPPER, TO TASTE

2 LEMONS, CUT INTO WEDGES, FOR SERVING

DIRECTIONS

1 Position a grate over the fire using gloved hands and tongs. Make sure the grate is as secure and level as possible.

2 Place the paprika, turmeric, onion powder, garlic powder, oregano, olive oil, vinegar, yogurt, and salt in a large bowl and whisk to combine.

3 Add the chicken pieces and stir until they are coated. Cover the bowl and let them marinate for at least 2 hours. If you have time, you can also let the chicken marinate overnight.

4 When the coals are glowing, warm a cast-iron grill pan for 10 minutes.

5 While the grill pan is heating up, thread the chicken onto skewers and season with salt and pepper.

6 Brush the pan with a light coating of olive oil and then add the chicken kebabs. Cook, while turning occasionally, until the chicken is golden brown and cooked through, approximately 10 minutes.

7 Serve warm or at room temperature with the lemon wedges.

Swedish Meatballs

YIELD: 4 TO 6 SERVINGS • ACTIVE TIME: 1 HOUR • TOTAL TIME: 1 HOUR AND 20 MINUTES

This is excellent with a side of buttered noodles or boiled and buttered new potatoes seasoned with dill, basil, or parsley. You can also serve it paired with lingonberry jam or red currant jelly.

INGREDIENTS

5 SLICES OF WHITE SANDWICH BREAD, CRUSTS REMOVED

¾ CUP WHOLE MILK

1½ LBS. GROUND BEEF

¾ LB. GROUND PORK

¼ LB. GROUND VEAL (OPTIONAL)

2 LARGE EGGS

2 TEASPOONS KOSHER SALT, PLUS MORE TO TASTE

1 TEASPOON NUTMEG

1 TEASPOON ALLSPICE

1 TEASPOON WHITE PEPPER

1 STICK OF UNSALTED BUTTER

1 SMALL YELLOW ONION, MINCED

¼ CUP ALL-PURPOSE FLOUR

4 CUPS BEEF STOCK

½ CUP SOUR CREAM

LINGONBERRY JAM OR RED CURRANT JELLY, FOR SERVING

DIRECTIONS

1 Position a grate over the fire using gloved hands and tongs. Make sure the grate is as secure and level as possible.

2 Tear the slices of bread into strips and place them in a bowl with the milk. Let the bread soak.

3 Place the meats, eggs, salt, nutmeg, allspice, and white pepper in a large bowl and use a wooden spoon or your hands to combine.

4 Remove the bread from the milk and squeeze to remove any excess liquid. Tear the bread into small pieces and stir into the meat mixture.

5 When the coals are glowing, melt 2 tablespoons of the butter in a 12-inch cast-iron skillet. Add the onion and sauté until it is translucent. Add the onion to the meat mixture and stir to combine.

6 Form the meat mixture into balls that are each about the size of a golf ball.

7 Place the remaining butter in the skillet and melt. Working in batches, add the meatballs to the skillet and cook, while turning frequently, until they are browned all over. Use a slotted spoon to remove the browned meatballs and set them aside.

8 Sprinkle the flour into the skillet and stir to incorporate. Add the stock 2 tablespoons at a time, while stirring, until it is emulsified. You should have a thick gravy in the skillet when all of the stock has been incorporated.

Continued...

9 Return the meatballs to the skillet, gently stir to coat with the sauce, and move the skillet to the edge of the fire. Cover the skillet and simmer for 10 minutes, turning the skillet every few minutes to avoid burn spots.

10 Stir in the sour cream or Crème Fraîche and serve with lingonberry jam or red currant jelly.

Veal Scallopini

YIELD: 4 SERVINGS • ACTIVE TIME: 15 MINUTES • TOTAL TIME: 20 MINUTES

This is an unexpected Italian preparation. The veal will get slightly crispy, exactly what you want alongside the meaty olives and the vibrant lemon juice. If you don't eat veal, try this with chicken.

INGREDIENTS

½ CUP ALL-PURPOSE FLOUR

½ TEASPOON NUTMEG

SALT AND PEPPER, TO TASTE

2 TABLESPOONS UNSALTED BUTTER

1 LB. VEAL CUTLETS (ABOUT 4), POUNDED THIN

½ CUP VEAL STOCK OR BEEF STOCK

¼ CUP GREEN OLIVES, SLICED

ZEST AND JUICE OF 1 LEMON

DIRECTIONS

1 Position a grate over the fire using gloved hands and tongs. Make sure the grate is as secure and level as possible.

2 When the coals are glowing, warm a 12-inch cast-iron skillet for 5 minutes.

3 Place the flour, nutmeg, salt, and pepper on a large plate and stir to combine.

4 Place the butter in the skillet. When it is sizzling, dredge the veal in the seasoned flour until they are coated lightly on both sides. Working in batches, place the veal in the skillet and cook for about 1 minute on each side, until it is browned and the juices run clear. Set the cooked veal aside.

5 Deglaze the pan with the stock. Add the olives, lemon zest, and lemon juice, stir to combine, and cook until heated through.

6 To serve, plate the veal and pour the pan sauce over each cutlet.

Irish Lamb Stew

YIELD: 4 SERVINGS • ACTIVE TIME: 30 MINUTES • TOTAL TIME: 2 HOURS AND 30 MINUTES

No food in this world can warm your soul more than this hearty, Old World–style stew containing tender lamb and root vegetables. Toast some thick slices of sourdough bread to serve alongside, and you've got the ideal antidote for a long day of outdoor activities.

INGREDIENTS

2 LBS. BONELESS LAMB SHOULDER, CUT INTO BITE-SIZED CUBES

2 BAY LEAVES

6 YUKON GOLD POTATOES, SLICED ¼-INCH THICK

3 YELLOW ONIONS, SLICED

2 LARGE RUTABAGAS, PEELED AND SLICED ¼-INCH THICK

SALT AND PEPPER, TO TASTE

4 SPRIGS FRESH PARSLEY

2 LARGE CARROTS, PEELED AND SLICED ½-INCH THICK

DIRECTIONS

1 Position a grate over the fire using gloved hands and tongs. Make sure the grate is as secure and level as possible. If using a tripod, set up prior to building your fire. You will need a round bottomed cauldron or a cast-iron Dutch oven with a hanging loop handle.

2 When the coals are glowing, place the lamb and bay leaves in a large cast-iron Dutch oven or a hanging cast-iron Dutch oven and cover with cold water. Bring to a boil over the center of the fire and cook for 5 minutes. Remove the lamb with a slotted spoon and set aside. Transfer the broth and bay leaves to a separate container.

3 Place half of the potatoes in a layer at the bottom of the Dutch oven. Top with a layer of half of the onions and another layer consisting of half of the rutabagas. Add the lamb, season with salt and pepper, and top with layers of the remaining potatoes, onions, and rutabagas. Add the broth and bay leaves and bring to a boil. Move the Dutch oven further from the center of the fire so that the stew simmers, cover, and cook for 1 hour, turning the Dutch oven every few minutes to avoid burn spots.

4 Remove the lid, add the parsley and carrots, and simmer for another hour. If not done, check every 15 minutes until cooked to your liking.

5 Remove the parsley and bay leaves and ladle the stew into warmed bowls.

Chicken & Vegetable Stew

YIELD: 6 SERVINGS • ACTIVE TIME: 15 TO 20 MINUTES • TOTAL TIME: 1 HOUR AND 45 MINUTES

A day's worth of protein, veggies, and flavor are packed into this stew—which requires minimal effort on your part.

INGREDIENTS

2 TABLESPOONS OLIVE OIL

2 LBS. CHICKEN THIGHS

SALT AND PEPPER, TO TASTE

1 WHITE ONION, DICED

3 CELERY STALKS, DICED

2 CARROTS, DICED

2 PARSNIPS, DICED

1 ZUCCHINI, DICED

1 YELLOW SQUASH, DICED

3 GARLIC CLOVES, MINCED

8 CUPS CHICKEN STOCK

2 BAY LEAVES

FRESH BASIL, CHOPPED, FOR GARNISH (OPTIONAL)

DIRECTIONS

1 Position a grate over the fire using gloved hands and tongs. Make sure the grate is as secure and level as possible. If using a tripod, set up prior to building your fire. You will need a round bottomed cauldron or a cast-iron Dutch oven with a hanging loop handle.

2 When the coals are glowing, place the olive oil in a cast-iron Dutch oven or a hanging cast-iron Dutch oven. Season the chicken thighs with salt and pepper and place them in the Dutch oven, skin side down. Cook for about 5 minutes on each side. Remove and set aside.

3 Add the onion, celery, carrots, and parsnips to the pot and cook for 5 to 7 minutes, until the onion starts to get translucent. Season with a pinch of salt and pepper and then add the zucchini, squash, and garlic. Cook for 5 minutes, while stirring, until the garlic is fragrant.

4 Season with salt and pepper and add the chicken thighs, stock, and bay leaves. Move the Dutch oven further from the center of the fire, cover, and cook for 1 hour or until the chicken is falling off the bone. Turn the Dutch oven every few minutes to avoid burn spots. If not done after 1 hour, check every 15 minutes until cooked to your liking. Season with salt and pepper to taste. Discard the bay leaves and, if desired, garnish with fresh basil before serving.

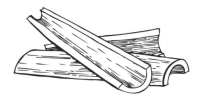

Thai Red Duck Curry

YIELD: 4 SERVINGS • ACTIVE TIME: 15 MINUTES • TOTAL TIME: 30 MINUTES

Your local store will likely have precooked duck breasts available for purchase, but it's worth cooking your own just to have access to the rich rendered fat that results from searing in cast iron.

INGREDIENTS

4 BONELESS, SKIN-ON DUCK BREASTS

¼ CUP THAI RED CURRY PASTE

2½ CUPS COCONUT MILK

10 MAKRUT LIME LEAVES (OPTIONAL)

1 CUP DICED PINEAPPLE

1 TABLESPOON FISH SAUCE, PLUS MORE TO TASTE

1 TABLESPOON BROWN SUGAR

6 BIRD'S EYE CHILIES, STEMMED

20 CHERRY TOMATOES

1 CUP BASIL (THAI BASIL STRONGLY PREFERRED)

1½ CUPS COOKED JASMINE RICE, FOR SERVING

DIRECTIONS

1 Position a grate over the fire using gloved hands and tongs. Make sure the grate is as secure and level as possible.

2 Use a very sharp knife to slash the skin on the duck breasts, while taking care not to cut all the way through to the meat.

3 When the coals are glowing, place a large cast-iron Dutch oven on the grate. Place the duck breasts, skin side down, in the pot and sear until browned, about 4 minutes. This will render a lot of the fat.

4 Turn the duck breasts over and cook until browned on the other side, about 4 minutes. Remove the duck from the pot, let cool, and drain the rendered duck fat. Reserve the duck fat for another use.

5 When the duck breasts are cool enough to handle, remove the skin and discard. Cut each breast into 2-inch pieces.

6 Move the Duth oven further from the center of the fire, add the curry paste, and fry for 2 minutes. Add the coconut milk, bring to a boil, and cook for 5 minutes.

7 Move the Dutch oven to the edge of the fire, return the duck to the pot, and simmer for 8 minutes. Add the lime leaves, if using, the pineapple, fish sauce, brown sugar, and chilies, stir to incorporate, and simmer for 5 minutes. Skim to remove any fat from the top as the curry simmers.

8 Taste and add more fish sauce if needed. Stir in the cherry tomatoes and basil and serve alongside the rice.

Pad Thai

YIELD: 4 SERVINGS • ACTIVE TIME: 15 MINUTES • TOTAL TIME: 35 MINUTES

You may be surprised that the most famous and popular Thai recipe is really very simple to make. The key is to balance the flavors properly so that you have a tangle of chewy noodles freighted with a delicious jumble of salty, sweet, sour, and spicy.

INGREDIENTS

6 OZ. THIN RICE NOODLES

2 CUPS BOILING WATER

3 TABLESPOONS VEGETABLE OIL

2 LARGE BONELESS, SKINLESS CHICKEN BREASTS, SLICED THIN

1 LARGE EGG

¼ CUP TAMARIND PASTE

2 TABLESPOONS WATER

1½ TABLESPOONS FISH SAUCE

2 TABLESPOONS RICE VINEGAR

1½ TABLESPOONS BROWN SUGAR

4 SCALLION GREENS, SLICED

1 CUP BEAN SPROUTS

½ TEASPOON CAYENNE PEPPER

¼ CUP PEANUTS, CRUSHED

2 LIMES, CUT INTO WEDGES, FOR SERVING

DIRECTIONS

1 Position a grate over the fire using gloved hands and tongs. Make sure the grate is as secure and level as possible.

2 Place the noodles in a wide, shallow bowl and pour the boiling water over them. Stir and let rest until they have softened, about 15 minutes.

3 When the coals are glowing, place the oil in a large cast-iron wok or 12-inch cast-iron skillet.

4 When the oil starts to shimmer, add the chicken and sauté until cooked through, about 5 minutes. Remove the chicken from the pan and set aside.

5 Add the egg to the pan and stir. Add the noodles and return the chicken to the pan. Stir to incorporate and then add the tamarind paste, water, fish sauce, vinegar, brown sugar, scallions, bean sprouts, cayenne pepper, and peanuts. Stir to combine and serve immediately with the lime wedges.

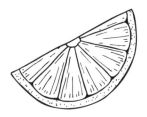

SEAFOOD

Seafood was practically made for the quick cooking and ample heat supplied by cast iron. It is the only material that can properly cook scallops, and its ability to crisp the skin of salmon adds another layer of loveliness to that rich fish. The campfire is perfect for exploring the incredible bounty provided by the ocean

Simple Skillet Salmon

YIELD: 4 TO 6 SERVINGS • ACTIVE TIME: 20 MINUTES • TOTAL TIME: 30 MINUTES

Start with super-fresh fish, and keep it simple—butter, lemon, salt, and pepper—and you can create a succulent dish that is ready in no time.

INGREDIENTS

3-4 LBS. SKIN-ON SALMON FILLETS

2 TABLESPOONS UNSALTED BUTTER, CUT INTO PIECES AND SOFTENED

1 LEMON, HALVED

SALT AND PEPPER, TO TASTE

1 TABLESPOON OLIVE OIL

DIRECTIONS

1 Position a grate over the fire using gloved hands and tongs. Make sure the grate is as secure and level as possible.

2 Rinse the fillets with cold water to ensure that any scales or bones are removed and pat them dry with paper towels. Rub the butter on both sides of the fillets, squeeze lemon over them, and season with salt and pepper.

3 When the coals are glowing, add the olive oil to a 12-inch cast-iron skillet. Add the fillets, flesh side down. Cook on one side for about 3 minutes, then flip them and cook for 2 minutes on the other side. Remove the skillet from heat and let the fish rest in it for a minute before serving. The skin should peel right off.

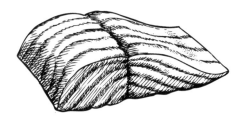

Cornmeal-Crusted Pollock with Rosemary Chips

YIELD: 2 TO 4 SERVINGS • ACTIVE TIME: 20 MINUTES • TOTAL TIME: 45 MINUTES

This New England twist on a British favorite is a must-try dish. Cook this up at the height of pollock season to really capture the essence of the fresh fish paired with the delicious cornmeal breading.

INGREDIENTS

4 CUPS CANOLA OIL

5 POTATOES, SLICED INTO LONG, THIN STRIPS

3 TABLESPOONS MINCED FRESH ROSEMARY LEAVES

SALT AND PEPPER, TO TASTE

2 EGGS, BEATEN

1 CUP CORNMEAL

1-1½ LBS. POLLOCK FILLETS

DIRECTIONS

1 Position a grate over the fire using gloved hands and tongs. Make sure the grate is as secure and level as possible.

2 When the coals are glowing, heat the canola oil in a cast-iron Dutch oven. If it starts to smoke, it is too hot.

3 When the oil is ready, place the sliced potatoes in the oil and cook until golden brown. Remove and set to drain on a paper towel–lined plate. Keep the oil hot.

4 When drained to your liking, place the fried potatoes in a bowl with the rosemary and salt and toss to coat. Set aside.

5 Place the beaten eggs in a small bowl and the cornmeal in another. Dip the pollock fillets into the egg and then into the cornmeal, repeating until coated all over.

6 Place the battered pollock in the oil and cook until golden brown. Remove and set to drain on another paper towel–lined plate. Serve with the rosemary chips.

Honey-Glazed Salmon

YIELD: 4 SERVINGS • ACTIVE TIME: 5 MINUTES • TOTAL TIME: 15 MINUTES

The rare recipe that is accessible for a beginner and still beloved by the most advanced chefs. The technique is straightforward and easy to master, and the results are nothing short of sublime. That it comes together in mere minutes is just another thing in its favor.

INGREDIENTS

4 SKIN-ON SALMON FILLETS

1 TABLESPOON OLIVE OIL

2 TABLESPOONS VEGETABLE OIL

KOSHER SALT, TO TASTE

3 TABLESPOONS HONEY

ZEST AND JUICE OF 1 LARGE LEMON

DIRECTIONS

1 Position a grate over the fire using gloved hands and tongs. Make sure the grate is as secure and level as possible.

2 Pat the salmon fillets dry with a paper towel. Rub the olive oil into them and season with salt.

3 When the coals are glowing, add the vegetable oil to a 12-inch cast-iron skillet. When it starts to shimmer, place the salmon fillets, skin side down, in the skillet and cook for 8 minutes.

4 Move the skillet further from the center of the fire and use a spatula to carefully flip the salmon fillets over. Cook for another 8 minutes.

5 While the salmon is cooking, place the honey, lemon zest, and lemon juice in a bowl and stir to combine.

6 When the salmon is cooked through, remove from the skillet, drizzle the honey glaze over the top, and serve.

Baked Cod with Lemons, Capers & Leeks

YIELD: 4 SERVINGS • ACTIVE TIME: 15 MINUTES • TOTAL TIME: 1 HOUR

The mild taste of cod pairs brilliantly with the bold flavors of lemon and capers.

INGREDIENTS

½ LB. LEEKS, TRIMMED AND RINSED WELL

SALT AND PEPPER, TO TASTE

2 TABLESPOONS OLIVE OIL

1½ LBS. COD FILLETS

2 TABLESPOONS FRESH LEMON JUICE

3 TABLESPOONS CAPERS

½ LEMON, SLICED THIN

LEMON WEDGES, FOR SERVING

DIRECTIONS

1 Position a grate over the fire using gloved hands and tongs. Make sure the grate is as secure and level as possible.

2 When the coals are glowing, pat the leeks dry, place them in a cast-iron Dutch oven, and season with salt and pepper. Cover the Dutch oven and roast until they start to brown, about 25 minutes, uncovering the pot halfway through.

3 Place the cod fillets on top of them, and sprinkle the lemon juice over the fish. Distribute the capers and slices of lemon over the cod fillets and cover the Dutch oven. Roast for 15 minutes, uncover, then roast for another 10 minutes, until the cod is cooked through and can be flaked with a fork. Serve with lemon wedges on the side.

Tea-Smoked Salmon

YIELD: 4 SERVINGS • ACTIVE TIME: 10 MINUTES • TOTAL TIME: 1 HOUR

Smoking food brings a whole different dimension of flavor that's totally worth exploring. A brief kiss can add a haunting flavor, while a long time in the smoker brings something wild and unctuous to the table.

INGREDIENTS

½ CUP VEGETABLE OIL, PLUS MORE AS NEEDED

½ CUP MIRIN

1 TABLESPOON BROWN SUGAR

1 TABLESPOON MINCED GINGER

1 TEASPOON ORANGE ZEST

1 LB. SKINLESS, CENTER-CUT SALMON FILLETS

1 CUP WHITE RICE

½ CUP GRANULATED SUGAR

1 CUP GREEN TEA (GUNPOWDER PREFERRED)

1 ORANGE PEEL, DICED

DIRECTIONS

1 Position a grate over the fire using gloved hands and tongs. Make sure the grate is as secure and level as possible.

2 In a shallow dish, whisk together the oil, mirin, brown sugar, ginger, and orange zest. Add the salmon and let marinate for 30 minutes.

3 When the coals are glowing, line a large cast-iron wok with foil. You want the foil to extend over the sides of the wok. Add the rice, granulated sugar, tea, and orange peel and cook over the center of the fire until the rice begins to smoke.

4 Place the salmon on a lightly oiled rack, set it above the smoking rice, and place the lid on top of wok. Fold the foil over the lid to seal the wok as best as you can.

5 Move the wok further from the center of the fire and cook for 10 minutes. If not done, check every few minutes until they are done to your liking.

6 Remove from heat and let the wok cool completely, about 20 minutes. When done, the fish will be cooked to medium. Serve immediately.

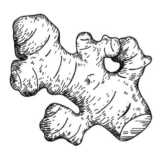

Blackened Tilapia

YIELD: 4 SERVINGS • ACTIVE TIME: 40 MINUTES • TOTAL TIME: 1 HOUR AND 30 MINUTES

The cast-iron skillet is perfect for blackening fish, which requires high heat and quick cooking. Tilapia is a wonderful fish for blackening, as it is a firm-fleshed fish that is fairly bland and thus benefits from generous seasoning. Although the result is delicious, the blackening process creates a lot of smoke, so beware before you start cooking.

INGREDIENTS

2 TABLESPOONS PAPRIKA

1 TABLESPOON ONION POWDER

3 TABLESPOONS GARLIC POWDER

2 TABLESPOONS CAYENNE PEPPER

1½ TEASPOONS CELERY SALT

1½ TABLESPOONS FINELY GROUND BLACK PEPPER

1 TABLESPOON DRIED THYME

1 TABLESPOON DRIED OREGANO

1 TABLESPOON CHIPOTLE POWDER

4 (4 OZ.) BONELESS TILAPIA FILLETS

1 STICK OF UNSALTED BUTTER, MELTED

1 LEMON, CUT INTO 4 WEDGES, FOR SERVING

DIRECTIONS

1 Position a grate over the fire using gloved hands and tongs. Make sure the grate is as secure and level as possible.

2 In a bowl, combine all the spices and set aside.

3 When the coals are glowing, place a 12-inch cast-iron skillet over the center of the fire for about 10 minutes until very hot. While the skillet heats up, rinse the fillets and then pat dry with paper towels. Dip the fillets in the melted butter, covering both sides, and then press the seasoning mixture generously into both sides.

4 Put the fish in the skillet and cook for about 3 minutes per side, placing a bit of butter on top while the other side is cooking. Serve with lemon wedges.

Linguine with Clam Sauce

YIELD: 4 TO 6 SERVINGS • ACTIVE TIME: 15 TO 20 MINUTES • TOTAL TIME: 30 TO 40 MINUTES

Easy, salty, and bursting with freshness. If you don't have much time but need to whip up something special, this dish won't let you down.

INGREDIENTS

1 LB. LINGUINE

2 TABLESPOONS SEA SALT

½ CUP OLIVE OIL

3 GARLIC CLOVES, SLICED THIN

32 LITTLENECK CLAMS, SCRUBBED AND RINSED

1 CUP WHITE WINE

1 CUP CLAM JUICE

1 CUP CHOPPED ITALIAN PARSLEY

¼ CUP GRATED PARMESAN CHEESE

SALT AND PEPPER, TO TASTE

DIRECTIONS

1 Position a grate over the fire using gloved hands and tongs. Make sure the grate is as secure and level as possible.

2 When the coals are glowing, bring 4 quarters of water to a boil in a cast-iron Dutch oven. Add the linguine and the sea salt. Cook for 7 minutes or until the pasta is just short of al dente. Drain, while reserving ½ cup of cooking water, and then set the linguine aside.

3 Place the Dutch oven back over the fire. Add half of the olive oil and all of the garlic to the pot and cook until the garlic starts to brown, about 2 minutes. Add the clams and wine, cover, and cook for 5 to 7 minutes or until the majority of the clams are open. Use a slotted spoon to transfer the clams to a colander. Discard any clams that do not open.

4 Add the clam juice, parsley, and pasta water to the Dutch oven. Cook until the sauce starts to thicken, about 10 minutes. Remove all the clams from their shells and mince one-quarter of them.

5 Return the linguine to the pot. Add the Parmesan, season with salt and pepper, and stir until the cheese begins to melt. Fold in the clams, drizzle with the remaining olive oil, and serve.

TIP: If you do not have access to fresh clams, you can use canned whole clams.

New England Lobster Rolls with Browned Buttermilk Crumbs

YIELD: 2 TO 4 SERVINGS • ACTIVE TIME: 10 MINUTES • TOTAL TIME: 25 MINUTES

Summer means seafood in New England, and no transformation of the ocean's bounty is more iconic than the lobster roll. This classic traditionally comes in one of two styles—either with mayonnaise or browned butter—and this recipe provides the best of both worlds.

INGREDIENTS

1 STICK OF UNSALTED BUTTER

1 CUP NONFAT MILK POWDER

2-4 HOT DOG OR HAMBURGER BUNS

MEAT FROM 2 TO 3 COOKED CHICKEN LOBSTERS

2 TABLESPOONS MAYONNAISE

SALT AND PEPPER, TO TASTE

DIRECTIONS

1 Position a grate over the fire using gloved hands and tongs. Make sure the grate is as secure and level as possible.

2 When the coals are glowing, melt the butter in a small saucepan on the edge of the grate.

3 When the butter is melted, stir in the milk powder and cook until the mixture starts to turn golden brown.

4 Remove the pan from heat and strain through a fine sieve over a bowl. Store the crumbs in an airtight container and reserve the browned butter.

5 Place the buns in a 12-inch cast-iron skillet with the reserved browned butter and cook for 1 minute on each side, until golden brown. Remove and set aside.

6 Place the lobster meat, mayonnaise, salt, and pepper in a mixing bowl and stir to combine.

7 Spoon the dressed lobster into the toasted buns, top with a generous amount of the browned buttermilk crumbs, and serve.

Clams with Chorizo

YIELD: 4 TO 6 SERVINGS • ACTIVE TIME: 15 MINUTES • TOTAL TIME: 15 MINUTES

Hailing from Spain's Basque country, this heady dish is as unique as the people who inhabit the region. Flavorful and light, it is perfect as part of a tapas-style meal.

INGREDIENTS

24 LITTLENECK CLAMS, SCRUBBED AND RINSED

1 TABLESPOON OLIVE OIL

1 YELLOW ONION, CHOPPED

3 GARLIC CLOVES, MINCED

2 CUPS CHERRY TOMATOES

2 OZ. SPANISH CHORIZO, MINCED

2 TABLESPOONS UNSALTED BUTTER, CUT INTO SMALL PIECES

DIRECTIONS

1 Position a grate over the fire using gloved hands and tongs. Make sure the grate is as secure and level as possible.

2 Pick over the clams and discard any that are open, cracked, or damaged.

3 When the coals are glowing, warm the olive oil in a 12-inch cast-iron skillet. When the oil starts to shimmer, add the onion and cook, without stirring, for 2 minutes. Add the garlic and tomatoes and cook, while stirring occasionally, until the tomatoes are browned and just beginning to burst, about 5 minutes. Add the chorizo, stir to incorporate, and cook for another 2 minutes.

4 Add the clams, cover the skillet, and let them steam until the majority of the clams have opened, about 2 minutes.

5 Remove any clams that haven't opened and discard. Add the butter and stir until the butter has melted. Serve warm or at room temperature.

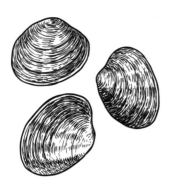

Garlic Shrimp

YIELD: 4 SERVINGS • ACTIVE TIME: 5 MINUTES • TOTAL TIME: 10 MINUTES

What's not to like here? Sweet, briny shrimp, loads of luscious butter, and a bit of mellowed garlic, all held together by the acidic kick of lemon. A culinary wonder that shines when made in cast iron.

INGREDIENTS

4 TABLESPOONS UNSALTED BUTTER, AT ROOM TEMPERATURE

1 LB. SHRIMP, PEELED AND DEVEINED

8 GARLIC CLOVES, MINCED

½ TEASPOON LEMON-PEPPER SEASONING

2 TEASPOONS FRESH LEMON JUICE

1 TEASPOON MINCED CHIVES OR PARSLEY, FOR GARNISH

1 RED CHILI PEPPER, SLICED THIN, FOR GARNISH (OPTIONAL)

DIRECTIONS

1 Position a grate over the fire using gloved hands and tongs. Make sure the grate is as secure and level as possible.

2 When the coals are glowing, add the butter to a 10-inch cast-iron skillet.

3 When the butter has melted and is foaming, add the shrimp and cook, without stirring, for 2 minutes. Remove from the pan and set aside.

4 Move the skillet further from the center of the fire and add the garlic and lemon-pepper seasoning. Cook until the garlic has softened, about 2 minutes. Return the shrimp to the pan and cook until warmed through, about 1 minute.

5 To serve, sprinkle with the lemon juice and garnish with the chives and chili pepper, if desired.

Walnut & Brown Butter Scallops with Butternut Squash

YIELD: 4 TO 6 SERVINGS • ACTIVE TIME: 40 MINUTES • TOTAL TIME: 1 HOUR AND 15 MINUTES

Here's another delicious and surprisingly simple recipe. If you are trying to impress someone, the combination of fresh, tender scallops and rich, nutty brown butter is a good start.

INGREDIENTS

24 JUMBO (U10) SCALLOPS

SALT AND PEPPER, TO TASTE

1 STICK OF UNSALTED BUTTER

2 TABLESPOONS OLIVE OIL

3-4 BUTTERNUT SQUASH, PEELED, SEEDED, AND DICED

1 CUP RAW, SHELLED WALNUTS

SCALLIONS, CHOPPED, FOR GARNISH

DIRECTIONS

1 Position a grate over the fire using gloved hands and tongs. Make sure the grate is as secure and level as possible.

2 When the coals are glowing, warm a 12-inch cast-iron skillet. Remove the foot from each scallop and discard. Pat the scallops dry with a paper towel and lightly season both sides with salt and pepper.

3 Place 1 tablespoon of the butter and the olive oil in the pan. Add the scallops one at a time, softly pressing down as you place them in the skillet. Cook the scallops for approximately 3 minutes and then flip them over. The scallops should not stick to the pan when you go to flip them. If the scallops do stick, cook until a brown crust is visible. Once you have flipped the scallops, cook for 2 minutes, remove, and set aside.

4 Add the butternut squash, season with salt and pepper, and cook for 12 to 15 minutes or until tender and caramelized. Remove the squash and set aside.

5 Add the walnuts to the pan and cook, while stirring often, for 2 minutes or until the nuts are fragrant. Add the remaining butter to the pan and cook for 2 to 3 minutes, until it has browned.

Continued...

6 Place the squash in the middle of a plate and then place the scallops around and on top of the squash. Spoon the walnuts and butter over the dish, garnish with the scallions, and serve.

TIPS: U10 is a unit of measurement that refers to the amount of scallops per pound, meaning that you will have 10 or fewer.

The foot of a scallop is a ½ x 1-inch milky white piece attached to the side. It can easily be peeled off.

VEGETABLES

⟶

Using your cast-iron cookware and campfire, you
can create truly masterful vegetable dishes that will appeal
to vegetarians, vegans, and meat-eaters alike.

Roasted Cauliflower Steaks

YIELD: 4 TO 6 SERVINGS • ACTIVE TIME: 30 MINUTES • TOTAL TIME: 1 HOUR

There's something about roasting cauliflower that accentuates its sweet, nutty flavor. Season it with warm, earthy spices like cumin and turmeric, and you have a delicious alternative to a starchy side, full of flavor and nutrition.

INGREDIENTS

1½ TABLESPOONS OLIVE OIL

1 TEASPOON SALT

FRESHLY GROUND BLACK PEPPER, TO TASTE

½ TEASPOON CUMIN

½ TEASPOON CORIANDER

½ TEASPOON TURMERIC

¼ TEASPOON CAYENNE PEPPER

1 HEAD OF CAULIFLOWER, TRIMMED

SOUR CREAM, FOR SERVING (OPTIONAL)

DIRECTIONS

1 Position a grate over the fire using gloved hands and tongs. Make sure the grate is as secure and level as possible.

2 In a bowl, combine the oil, salt, pepper, and spices and whisk to mix thoroughly.

3 Cut the cauliflower crosswise into ½-inch slices. Put the slices in a 12-inch cast-iron skillet and brush the tops liberally with the oil mixture. Turn the "steaks" over and brush the other side.

4 When the coals are glowing, cover the skillet and roast for about 10 minutes. Turn the pieces over, uncover the skillet, and roast for another 10. A toothpick inserted in the flesh should go in easily to indicate that the cauliflower is cooked through.

5 Serve the slices hot, with a side of sour cream, if desired.

TIP: This recipe can be made with cauliflower florets, too. Instead of slicing the cauliflower into cross sections, just pick off the florets. Put them in the bowl of seasoned oil and toss to coat. Put the florets in the skillet and bake, shaking the pan halfway through to turn the pieces.

Blistered Shishito Peppers

YIELD: 4 TO 6 SERVINGS • ACTIVE TIME: 5 MINUTES • TOTAL TIME: 10 MINUTES

Shishito peppers are slightly twisted, bright green, and utterly delicious. Eating them is a bit like putting your taste buds through a round of Russian roulette, since approximately one in every 10 is spicy, and there's no way to tell until you bite down. The rest are as mild as can be. If you can't find shishitos, you can easily substitute padrón peppers.

INGREDIENTS

OLIVE OIL, FOR FRYING

2 LBS. SHISHITO PEPPERS

MALDON SEA SALT, TO TASTE

1 LEMON, CUT INTO WEDGES, FOR SERVING

DIRECTIONS

1 Position a grate over the fire using gloved hands and tongs. Make sure the grate is as secure and level as possible.

2 When the coals are glowing, add the olive oil to a 12-inch cast-iron skillet until it is ½-inch deep and warm.

3 When the oil is shimmering, add the peppers and cook, while turning once or twice, until they are blistered and golden brown, about 2 minutes. Take care not to crowd the peppers in the pan, and work in batches if necessary.

4 Transfer the blistered peppers to a paper towel–lined plate. Season with salt and serve with lemon wedges.

Crispy & Tender Asparagus

YIELD: 4 SERVINGS • ACTIVE TIME: 20 MINUTES • TOTAL TIME: 30 MINUTES

When making asparagus in a skillet, the outside gets crisp while the inside becomes tender. The thinner the asparagus, the faster the stalks will cook, so if you are working with super-fresh, thin stalks, you may need to reduce the cooking times in the recipe.

INGREDIENTS

3 TABLESPOONS OLIVE OIL

1 BUNCH OF THIN ASPARAGUS, WOODY ENDS REMOVED

1 GARLIC CLOVE, MINCED

½ TEASPOON SALT

½ TEASPOON FRESHLY GROUND BLACK PEPPER

LEMON WEDGES, FOR SERVING

DIRECTIONS

1 Position a grate over the fire using gloved hands and tongs. Make sure the grate is as secure and level as possible.

2 When the coals are glowing, place a 12-inch cast-iron skillet over the grate. When hot, add the oil and let that get hot. Add the asparagus. Using tongs, keep turning them so they cook evenly in the oil. Cook the asparagus until they are bright green and hot on the outside but tender on the inside.

3 Add the garlic, salt, and pepper, and shake the pan to distribute evenly. Cook for another 2 minutes. Transfer to a serving platter and serve with lemon wedges.

Roasted Root Vegetables

YIELD: 4 TO 6 SERVINGS • ACTIVE TIME: 20 MINUTES • TOTAL TIME: 1 HOUR

If you find yourself with bunches of root vegetables that looked so good at the farmers market but are now baffling you as a cook, this recipe is here to save the day.

INGREDIENTS

2 SMALL PARSNIPS, TRIMMED, SCRUBBED, AND CUT INTO BATONS

1 TURNIP, TRIMMED, SCRUBBED, AND CUT INTO BATONS

4 SMALL BEETS, TRIMMED, SCRUBBED, AND CUT INTO BATONS

4 CARROTS, TRIMMED, SCRUBBED, AND CUT INTO BATONS

½ ONION, SLICED

1 SMALL BULB FENNEL, TRIMMED AND CUT INTO MATCHSTICKS

¼ CUP OLIVE OIL

SALT AND PEPPER, TO TASTE

2 TEASPOONS DRIED ROSEMARY

DIRECTIONS

1 Position a grate over the fire using gloved hands and tongs. Make sure the grate is as secure and level as possible.

2 In a large bowl, combine all the vegetables and pour the olive oil over them. Season with salt and pepper and toss to coat.

3 When the coals are glowing, put the vegetables in a 12-inch cast-iron skillet and sprinkle the rosemary over everything.

4 Cover the skillet and roast for about 20 minutes. Turn the vegetables, uncover the skillet, and cook for another 20 minutes. Serve warm.

VARIATION: Substitute Herbes de Provence for the rosemary. This is a French blend of rosemary, fennel, basil, thyme, marjoram, basil, tarragon, and lavender—all the goodness of a Provençal herb garden.

Marvelous Mushrooms

YIELD: 4 SERVINGS • ACTIVE TIME: 20 MINUTES • TOTAL TIME: 30 MINUTES

There are many kinds of mushrooms available, and you can mix and match them as you desire. Sautéing mushrooms in the skillet with lots of butter yields a rich, earthy stew that is delicious with steak and potatoes. Or simply serve these mushrooms as a topping for burgers or baked polenta with cheese.

INGREDIENTS

6 TABLESPOONS UNSALTED BUTTER, CUT INTO SMALL PIECES

1 LB. MUSHROOMS, SLICED

1 TEASPOON DRY VERMOUTH

SALT AND PEPPER, TO TASTE

DIRECTIONS

1 Position a grate over the fire using gloved hands and tongs. Make sure the grate is as secure and level as possible.

2 When the coals are glowing, add the butter to a 12-inch cast-iron skillet. When melted, add the mushrooms. Cook, while stirring, until the mushrooms begin to soften, about 5 minutes. Move the skillet to the edge of the fire and let the mushrooms simmer, stirring occasionally, until they cook down, about 15 to 20 minutes.

3 Add the vermouth and stir, then season with salt and pepper. Simmer until the mushrooms are tender. Serve hot.

Creamed Pearl Onions

YIELD: 8 SERVINGS • ACTIVE TIME: 35 MINUTES • TOTAL TIME: 35 MINUTES

A rich, comforting dish that is right at home beside a roasted chicken or turkey. Fresh pearl onions are ideal, but in the interest of saving time, you can use frozen pearl onions. They come in red or white, and a mix of the two makes for a visually stunning presentation. If you're lucky to live in an area where shallots are abundant, don't hesitate to toss a few of those in, too.

INGREDIENTS

2½ TABLESPOONS UNSALTED BUTTER

2 TABLESPOONS ALL-PURPOSE FLOUR

1½ CUPS VEGETABLE STOCK OR CHICKEN STOCK

½ CUP HEAVY CREAM, AT ROOM TEMPERATURE

½ CUP DRY WHITE WINE

¼ TEASPOON GROUND DRIED SAGE

1 LB. FROZEN PEARL ONIONS, THAWED AND DRAINED

SALT AND PEPPER, TO TASTE

DIRECTIONS

1 Position a grate over the fire using gloved hands and tongs. Make sure the grate is as secure and level as possible.

2 When the coals are glowing, place 2 tablespoons of the butter in a 12-inch cast-iron skillet and melt. Add the flour and cook, while stirring constantly, until it is golden brown, about 6 minutes. Gradually whisk in the stock and bring to a boil, whisking until the roux is smooth. Remove the skillet from heat and whisk in the cream.

3 Place the skillet back over the fire and cook, while stirring frequently, until the sauce thickens, about 8 minutes.

4 Add the wine and sage and cook, while stirring, until the sauce has further thickened, about 2 minutes.

5 Add the onions and move the skillet further from the center of the fire. Cook, while stirring frequently, until all of the onions are warmed through, about 6 minutes.

6 Whisk in the remaining butter, season with salt and pepper, and serve immediately.

Charred Onion Petals

An easy-to-master and utterly beautiful preparation that makes for a stunning side dish. Make sure to use sweet onions, though, since the flavor of yellow onions will be too sharp. These are just as good cold, so don't hesitate to make a batch ahead of time.

INGREDIENTS

3 SWEET ONIONS (MAUI OR VIDALIA)

2 TABLESPOONS VEGETABLE OIL

FLAKY SEA SALT, TO TASTE

DIRECTIONS

1 Position a grate over the fire using gloved hands and tongs. Make sure the grate is as secure and level as possible.

2 Cut each onion in half lengthwise and remove the outer layer.

3 When the coals are glowing, place a 12-inch cast-iron skillet close to the center of the fire and add the vegetable oil. When the oil is shimmering, place the onions, cut side down, in the pan. Move the skillet further from the center of the fire and cook until the onions are charred, about 20 minutes. They will smell burnt, but don't worry.

4 Cover the skillet and roast for about 5-7 minutes, then uncover and roast for another 5-7 minutes, until the onions are tender. Let the onions cool.

5 When the onions are cool enough to handle, use kitchen scissors to trim the tops and roots. Discard and separate the layers into individual petals. Season with salt and serve.

Creamed Kale & Swiss Chard

YIELD: 4 SERVINGS • ACTIVE TIME: 5 MINUTES • TOTAL TIME: 20 MINUTES

This dish is a brassica lover's dream, and it will change the mind of anyone who doesn't love their greens. The mustard powder pulls double duty here, adding a burst of flavor and helping to thicken the sauce. If you can find rainbow chard, use that: the pretty red-and-yellow stems will make the dish Insta-worthy.

INGREDIENTS

2 TABLESPOONS COCONUT OIL

4 CUPS SHREDDED KALE LEAVES

2 TEASPOONS MUSTARD POWDER

1 CUP HEAVY CREAM

¼ CUP WATER

1 LARGE BUNCH OF SWISS CHARD, LEAVES AND STEMS CHOPPED

SALT, TO TASTE

DIRECTIONS

1 Position a grate over the fire using gloved hands and tongs. Make sure the grate is as secure and level as possible.

2 When the coals are glowing, warm the coconut oil in a large cast-iron Dutch oven.

3 When the oil is shimmering, add the kale and stir to coat. Cook until the greens are wilted, about 5 minutes.

4 Add the mustard powder, cream, and water. Stir to incorporate, move the Dutch oven further from the center of the fire, and simmer for 5 minutes.

5 Remove the lid and stir in the Swiss chard. Cover again and simmer until the chard is wilted, about 2 minutes. Season with salt and serve.

Roasted Garlic Radicchio

YIELD: 4 SERVINGS • ACTIVE TIME: 10 MINUTES • TOTAL TIME: 1 HOUR AND 30 MINUTES

If you like tart and bitter vegetables, this dish is for you. Just make sure the skillet is screaming hot before you add the radicchio, since you want it to be charred before adding the rest of the marinade.

INGREDIENTS

¼ CUP OLIVE OIL

8 GARLIC CLOVES, MINCED

2 TEASPOONS MINCED ROSEMARY LEAVES

¼ CUP BALSAMIC VINEGAR

1 ANCHOVY FILLET, SMASHED (OPTIONAL)

SALT AND PEPPER, TO TASTE

4 HEADS OF RADICCHIO, HALVED THROUGH THE ROOT

PARMESAN CHEESE, GRATED, FOR GARNISH

DIRECTIONS

1 Position a grate over the fire using gloved hands and tongs. Make sure the grate is as secure and level as possible.

2 Place the olive oil, garlic, rosemary, vinegar, anchovy (if using), salt, and pepper in a large bowl and stir to combine. Add the radicchio to the bowl and carefully toss to coat. Let the radicchio marinate for 1 hour.

3 When the coals are glowing, place a 12-inch cast-iron skillet over the center of the fire for 10 minutes, until it is extremely hot. Using tongs, remove the radicchio from the marinade and arrange, cut side down, in the skillet. Let it sear for a few minutes.

4 Move the skillet further away from the center of the fire and pour the marinade over the radicchio. Cover and roast for about 10 minutes, then uncover and roast for another 10, until the radicchio is tender. Remove and garnish with the Parmesan before serving.

Spinach & Shallots

YIELD: 6 TO 8 SERVINGS • ACTIVE TIME: 10 MINUTES • TOTAL TIME: 10 MINUTES

Using mellow-flavored shallots instead of the usual garlic and onions keeps the spinach flavor bright in this quick-cooking dish. A splash of balsamic vinegar takes it over the top.

INGREDIENTS

3 TABLESPOONS OLIVE OIL

4 LARGE SHALLOTS, SLICED THIN

2 LBS. FRESH SPINACH, STEMMED, RINSED, AND THOROUGHLY DRIED

1 TABLESPOON BALSAMIC VINEGAR

SALT AND PEPPER, TO TASTE

DIRECTIONS

1 Position a grate over the fire using gloved hands and tongs. Make sure the grate is as secure and level as possible.

2 When the coals are glowing, place a 12-inch cast-iron skillet over the fire. Add the olive oil and shallots and cook, while stirring, until shallots are translucent, about 2 minutes.

3 Add the spinach and cook, while stirring, until the leaves are covered by the oil and shallots, about 2 or 3 minutes. The spinach will start to wilt quickly. Move the skillet further away from the center of the fire and keep stirring so none of it burns. If desired, you can move the skillet to the edge of the fire and cover so the spinach steams.

4 When the spinach leaves are wilted and still bright green, splash them with the balsamic vinegar, shaking the skillet to distribute. Season with salt and pepper and serve.

VARIATIONS: This dish works best with more mature spinach. Reserve baby spinach greens for salads and use the larger leaves for this dish. If you prefer a less onion-y dish, use two shallots instead of four.

Stuffed Tomatoes

YIELD: 6 SERVINGS • ACTIVE TIME: 1 HOUR • TOTAL TIME: 2 HOURS

If you want to make this without sausage, simply omit it, double the quantity of mushrooms, and, after sautéing the mushrooms and peppers, drain the excess liquid. You can also add toasted walnut pieces for additional flavor and fiber.

INGREDIENTS

6 LARGE RIPE TOMATOES

SALT AND PEPPER, TO TASTE

1 LB. SAUSAGE, CASINGS REMOVED

1 ONION, DICED

4 GARLIC CLOVES, MINCED

8 WHITE MUSHROOMS, STEMMED AND DICED

½ GREEN BELL PEPPER, SEEDED AND DICED

2 TEASPOONS RED PEPPER FLAKES (OPTIONAL)

2 CUPS PLAIN BREAD CRUMBS

2 TABLESPOONS DRIED SAGE

1 CUP GRATED PARMESAN CHEESE

OLIVE OIL, AS NEEDED

DIRECTIONS

1 Position a grate over the fire using gloved hands and tongs. Make sure the grate is as secure and level as possible.

2 Cut off the tops of the tomatoes, and use a small paring knife or a serrated grapefruit spoon to scoop out the insides. Once hollowed, sprinkle salt on the insides and turn upside down on a plate covered with a paper towel to absorb the water. Let sit for about 30 minutes.

3 When the coals are glowing, heat a cast-iron Dutch oven and cook the sausage, breaking it up with a wooden spoon as it cooks. Cook until there is no pink showing in the meat. When cooked, use a slotted spoon to transfer the sausage to a large bowl. In the sausage fat, cook the onion and garlic until the onion is translucent, about 4 minutes. Add the mushrooms and bell pepper and cook, while stirring, until vegetables soften, about 10 minutes. Add red pepper flakes, if desired.

4 Add the mushroom mixture to the sausage and stir to combine. Then add the bread crumbs, sage, and Parmesan. Season with salt and pepper.

5 Wipe down the Dutch oven and brush with olive oil. Position the tomatoes in the Dutch oven, bottoms down. Start filling the tomatoes gently, dividing the filling between them. Cover the Dutch oven and bake for about 30 minutes, turning the Dutch oven every few minutes to avoid burn spots. Remove the lid, and continue baking for another 10 to 15 minutes, until cooked through. Serve hot.

Fried Artichokes with Gremolata

YIELD: 2 TO 4 SERVINGS • ACTIVE TIME: 20 MINUTES • TOTAL TIME: 30 MINUTES

This beautiful dish is one of the classics in Roman Jewish cuisine, where it is known as carciofi alla giudia. Like so many culinary cornerstones, it's simple: fry tender artichokes until crisp and dress with an Italian gremolata. The key is seasoning the artichokes with the correct amount of salt after they come out of the oil, so don't be afraid to experiment until you get it just right.

INGREDIENTS

ZEST AND JUICE OF 2 LARGE LEMONS

2 CUPS WATER

½ CUP MINCED PARSLEY

7 GARLIC CLOVES, 6 MINCED, 1 WHOLE

3 LBS. BABY ARTICHOKES, TRIMMED

OLIVE OIL, FOR FRYING

SALT, TO TASTE

DIRECTIONS

1 Position a grate over the fire using gloved hands and tongs. Make sure the grate is as secure and level as possible.

2 Place the lemon zest in a small bowl. Place the lemon juice in a separate bowl. Add the water to the lemon juice, stir to combine, and set aside.

3 Add the parsley and the minced garlic to the lemon zest, stir to combine, and set the gremolata aside.

4 Cut any large artichokes in half lengthwise. Place all of the artichokes in the lemon water. Line a plate with paper towels and set it aside.

5 When the coals are glowing, add olive oil to a cast-iron Dutch oven until it is ½-inch deep. Warm for 4 minutes and then drop in the whole garlic clove. Remove the garlic when the oil starts to bubble.

6 Drain the artichokes and pat dry. Working in three batches, drop the artichokes into the oil and fry, while turning occasionally, until golden brown, about 5 minutes. Carefully remove the fried artichokes and transfer them to the lined plate. Sprinkle with salt, garnish with the gremolata, and serve.

Roasted Sunchokes

YIELD: 4 SERVINGS • ACTIVE TIME: 10 MINUTES • TOTAL TIME: 40 MINUTES

Slow roasting is required to draw out the sweet and nutty flavor of sunchokes—also known as Jerusalem artichokes. Adding a small amount of water to the pan is the key when slow-roasting vegetables, as it keeps them from drying out as they brown. Serve this alongside chicken, beef, rabbit, or lamb.

INGREDIENTS

2 LBS. SUNCHOKES, SCRUBBED

1 TABLESPOON OLIVE OIL

KOSHER SALT, TO TASTE

¼ CUP WATER

DIRECTIONS

1 Position a grate over the fire using gloved hands and tongs. Make sure the grate is as secure and level as possible.

2 Place the sunchokes and olive oil in a large bowl and toss to coat. Season with salt and toss to coat.

3 When the coals are glowing, warm a 12-inch cast-iron skillet over the center of the fire. When it is hot, add the sunchokes and water, cover, and roast for 20 minutes. Stir and then cook, uncovered, for another 15 minutes, until the sunchokes are well-browned and tender.

Edamame Succotash

YIELD: 4 TO 6 SERVINGS • ACTIVE TIME: 5 MINUTES • TOTAL TIME: 20 MINUTES

Everyone knows that "succotash" is fun to say, but many have never tried the dish that has proven to be such a lexical delight. Maybe that's because of the divisive lima beans that feature in traditional preparations. We decided to switch those out for protein-rich and bright edamame, making this side dish a welcome sight at any campsite.

INGREDIENTS

4 SLICES OF THICK-CUT BACON

1 RED ONION, MINCED

KERNELS FROM 5 EARS OF CORN (ABOUT 4 CUPS)

1 RED BELL PEPPER, SEEDED AND DICED

1 CUP CANNED BLACK BEANS (OPTIONAL)

2 CUPS FRESH OR FROZEN EDAMAME

1 TABLESPOON UNSALTED BUTTER

SALT AND PEPPER, TO TASTE

1 TABLESPOON MINCED FRESH MARJORAM OR OREGANO

½ CUP CHOPPED FRESH BASIL

DIRECTIONS

1 Position a grate over the fire using gloved hands and tongs. Make sure the grate is as secure and level as possible.

2 When the coals are glowing, add the bacon to a 12-inch cast-iron skillet and cook until crispy, about 8 minutes. Remove from the pan and place on a paper towel–lined plate to drain. When it is cool enough to handle, crumble into bite-sized pieces.

3 Wipe the excess drippings from the skillet and add the onion. Cook until it has softened, about 5 minutes. Add the corn, bell pepper, black beans (if using), and edamame and cook, while stirring often, until the corn is tender and bright yellow, about 4 minutes.

4 Add the butter and stir until it has melted and everything is evenly coated. Season with salt and pepper.

5 Add the marjoram or oregano, basil, and crumbled bacon, stir to incorporate, and serve.

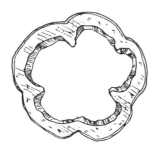

Green Beans with Bacon

YIELD: 4 SERVINGS • ACTIVE TIME: 10 MINUTES • TOTAL TIME: 15 MINUTES

As contemporary culture continually asserts, you can never go wrong with bacon. Smoky, salty, and buttery, the balance of flavors it possesses is unmatched. Here it is charged with lifting green beans to transcendent heights, a task it handles beautifully.

INGREDIENTS

6 SLICES OF UNCURED BACON

2 CUPS TRIMMED GREEN BEANS

SALT AND PEPPER, TO TASTE

DIRECTIONS

1 Position a grate over the fire using gloved hands and tongs. Make sure the grate is as secure and level as possible.

2 When the coals are glowing, heat a 12-inch cast-iron skillet for 5 minutes, until it is hot. Add the bacon and cook until it is browned, about 6 minutes. Transfer to a paper towel–lined plate to drain. When cool enough to handle, crumble into bite-sized pieces.

3 Remove all but 2 tablespoons of the bacon drippings from the skillet. Add the green beans and sauté, while tossing to coat, for about 4 minutes. The green beans should be bright green and just tender. Remove from the skillet and season with salt and pepper.

4 Sprinkle the crumbled bacon on top and serve.

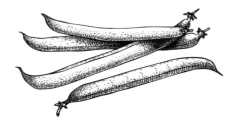

Ratatouille

YIELD: 4 SERVINGS • ACTIVE TIME: 40 MINUTES • TOTAL TIME: 2 HOURS

There are variations on this dish—some insist that zucchini is a necessary ingredient—but this recipe calls for just eggplant, peppers, and tomatoes (and garlic, of course) for a simple, filling meal.

INGREDIENTS

⅓ CUP OLIVE OIL, PLUS MORE AS NEEDED

6 GARLIC CLOVES, MINCED

1 EGGPLANT, TRIMMED AND CUT INTO BITE-SIZED CUBES

2 BELL PEPPERS, SEEDED AND DICED

4 TOMATOES, SEEDED AND CHOPPED

SALT AND PEPPER, TO TASTE

DIRECTIONS

1 Position a grate over the fire using gloved hands and tongs. Make sure the grate is as secure and level as possible.

2 When the coals are glowing, heat half of the olive oil in a 12-inch cast-iron skillet. Add the garlic and eggplant and cook, while stirring, until the pieces are coated with oil and just starting to sizzle, about 2 minutes. Move the skillet slightly further away from the center of the fire, add the peppers and remaining oil, and stir to combine. Cover the skillet and let cook, stirring every few minutes to be sure vegetables aren't sticking to the bottom of the pan. If the mix seems too dry, add a little more olive oil. As the eggplant softens, the dish will regain moisture.

3 After about 15 minutes, when the eggplant and peppers are nearly soft, add the tomatoes and stir to combine. With the lid off, continue to cook the ratatouille, stirring occasionally, until the eggplant and peppers are soft and the tomatoes are wilted. Remove the skillet from heat, season with salt and pepper, and allow to sit for at least 1 hour. Reheat before serving.

VARIATION: If you want to make this with zucchini, choose a small one, and cut it into thin half-moons. Add the zucchini with the peppers.

DESSERTS

Cooking over a campfire doesn't mean you have to skip on dessert. In fact, some of your favorite desserts are even more delicious when made in cast iron. This chapter introduces you to the decadent desserts you can enjoy outside the conventional kitchen.

Baked Crust

Many of the pies in this book call for a simple, single baked crust. It's fast and easy to put together and the result is delicious.

INGREDIENTS

1¼ CUPS ALL-PURPOSE FLOUR, PLUS MORE FOR DUSTING

¼ TEASPOON SALT

1 STICK OF UNSALTED BUTTER, CHILLED AND CUT INTO SMALL PIECES, PLUS 1 TABLESPOON FOR GREASING THE SKILLET

4-6 TABLESPOONS ICE WATER

DIRECTIONS

1 In a large bowl, combine the flour and salt. Add the stick of butter and work it into the flour mixture with a pastry blender or 2 knives until the dough resembles coarse meal. Add 3 tablespoons cold water to start, and, using your hands or a fork, work the dough, adding additional tablespoons of water until the dough just holds together when you gather it in your hands.

2 Working on a lightly floured surface, gather the dough and form it into a solid ball or disk. Wrap tightly in plastic wrap and chill for about an hour. The dough can be kept in a cooler for a couple of days.

3 Position a grate over the fire using gloved hands and tongs. Make sure the grate is as secure and level as possible. Take the dough out of the cooler to allow it to warm up a bit, but work with it cold. Put the chilled dough on a lightly floured surface, and, with a lightly dusted rolling pin, flatten the dough into a circle, working to extend it to a 12-inch round.

4 Grease a 12-inch cast-iron skillet with the remaining tablespoon of butter.

5 Carefully position the crust in the skillet so it is evenly distributed, pressing it in lightly. Crimp the edges. Use a fork to prick the crust on the bottom and sides. Line with foil or parchment paper and fill with uncooked rice as a weight.

6 When the coals are glowing, cover and bake for 10 to 12 minutes, or until lightly browned, turning the skillet every few minutes to avoid burn spots. Transfer to a wire rack to cool before filling.

Flaky Pastry Crust

YIELD: 2 12-INCH CRUSTS • ACTIVE TIME: 30 MINUTES • TOTAL TIME: 2 TO 3 HOURS

This is a traditional pie crust recipe, and while it's tempting to take a shortcut and use a mix or even a premade crust, there truly is nothing as delicious as a crust made from scratch. Once you get the hang of it, you'll find making the crust as enjoyable and therapeutic as indulging in the pie.

INGREDIENTS

2½ CUPS ALL-PURPOSE FLOUR, PLUS MORE FOR DUSTING

1¼ TEASPOONS SALT

¼ CUP VEGETABLE SHORTENING

1 STICK OF UNSALTED BUTTER, CHILLED AND CUT INTO SMALL PIECES, PLUS 1 TABLESPOON FOR GREASING THE SKILLET

6-8 TABLESPOONS COLD WATER

DIRECTIONS

1 In a large bowl, combine the flour and salt. Add the shortening, and, using a fork, work it in until the mixture forms a very coarse meal. Add the stick of butter and work it into the dough with a pastry blender or your fingers until the butter is incorporated. Don't overwork the dough; there can be chunks of butter in it. Add 4 tablespoons cold water to start, and, using your hands or a fork, work the dough, adding additional tablespoons of water until the dough just holds together when you gather it in your hands.

2 Working on a lightly floured surface, gather the dough and form it into a solid ball. Separate into equal parts and form into disks. Wrap each tightly in plastic wrap and put in the cooler for 30 minutes to 1 hour. Dough can be kept in the cooler for a couple of days.

3 Take the dough out of the cooler to allow it to warm up a bit, but work with it cold. Put the chilled dough on a lightly floured surface, and, with a lightly dusted rolling pin, flatten the dough into 2 circles, working to extend each to a 12-inch round.

4 Grease a 12-inch cast-iron skillet with the remaining tablespoon of butter.

5 Carefully position the crust in the covered skillet so it is evenly distributed, pressing it in lightly.

Continued...

6 If making a single-crust pie, crimp the edges as desired. If filling and adding a top crust, leave the extra dough so it can be crimped with the top crust. Fill the pie as directed, and then roll out the top crust so it is just bigger than the diameter of the other pie crust. For an extra-flaky pastry crust, chill the assembled pie for about 30 minutes before baking.

7 When the coals are glowing and you are ready to bake, cut a slit or hole in the middle of the top crust for heat and water vapor to escape. Brush the crust with milk, which will turn it a nice brown color. Bake as directed.

Sweet & Savory Cornmeal Crust

YIELD: 10-INCH CRUST • ACTIVE TIME: 20 MINUTES • TOTAL TIME: 1 HOUR AND 30 MINUTES

A crust that includes cornmeal will have more texture and flavor than a crust made from solely all-purpose flour. The distinctive texture and flavor are the perfect complements to savory fillings when prepared without sugar, but this makes a great base for sweet pies as well.

INGREDIENTS

¾ CUP ALL-PURPOSE FLOUR, PLUS MORE FOR DUSTING

¾ CUP YELLOW CORNMEAL

3 TABLESPOONS SUGAR (IF MAKING A SWEET CRUST)

½ TEASPOON SALT

1 STICK OF UNSALTED BUTTER, CHILLED AND CUT INTO SMALL PIECES, PLUS 1 TABLESPOON FOR GREASING THE SKILLET

1 EGG, LIGHTLY BEATEN

DIRECTIONS

1 In a large bowl, thoroughly combine the flour, cornmeal, sugar if making a sweet crust, and salt. Add the stick of butter and work it into the flour mixture with a pastry blender or your fingers to form a coarse meal. Add the egg and continue to blend until the dough comes together.

2 Shape into a disk, cover tightly with plastic wrap, and put in the cooler for 30 minutes.

3 Position a grate over the fire using gloved hands and tongs. Make sure the grate is as secure and level as possible. Take the dough out of the cooler to allow it to warm up a bit, but work with it cold. Put the chilled dough on a lightly floured surface, and, with a lightly dusted rolling pin, flatten the dough into a circle, working to extend it to a 10-inch round.

4 Grease a 10-inch cast-iron skillet with the remaining tablespoon of butter.

5 Carefully position the crust in the skillet so it is evenly distributed, pressing it in lightly. Crimp the edges. Use a fork to prick the crust on the bottom and sides. Line with foil or parchment paper, and fill with uncooked rice as a weight.

6 When the coals are glowing, cover and bake for 10 to 12 minutes, or until lightly browned, turning the skillet every few minutes to avoid burn spots. Transfer to a wire rack to cool before filling.

Graham Cracker Crust

YIELD: 10-INCH CRUST • ACTIVE TIME: 20 MINUTES • TOTAL TIME: 45 MINUTES

You can crush graham crackers to make this crust, or you can purchase graham cracker crumbs in the baked goods aisle of your grocery store. Either works, as the cracker is held together with butter and sugar. There are so many fillings that complement the flavor and texture of a graham cracker crust, so be sure to experiment and enjoy.

INGREDIENTS

1½ CUPS GRAHAM CRACKER CRUMBS

2 TABLESPOONS SUGAR

1 TABLESPOON MAPLE SYRUP

5 TABLESPOONS UNSALTED BUTTER, MELTED, PLUS 1 TABLESPOON AT ROOM TEMPERATURE FOR GREASING THE SKILLET

DIRECTIONS

1 Position a grate over the fire using gloved hands and tongs. Make sure the grate is as secure and level as possible.

2 In a large bowl, add the graham cracker crumbs and sugar and stir to combine. Add the maple syrup and melted butter and stir to thoroughly combine.

3 Liberally grease a 10-inch cast-iron skillet with the tablespoon of room-temperature butter. Pour the dough into the skillet and lightly press into shape. Line with aluminum foil and fill with uncooked rice as a weight. When the coals are glowing, cover and bake for 10 to 12 minutes, or until golden, turning the skillet every few minutes to avoid burn spots.

4 Allow to cool on a wire rack before filling.

Blueberry Pie

YIELD: 6 TO 8 SERVINGS • ACTIVE TIME: 1 HOUR • TOTAL TIME: 2 HOURS

An incredibly easy way to capture the brief glory that is blueberry season. It's summer in a slice!

INGREDIENTS

4 CUPS FRESH OR FROZEN BLUEBERRIES

1 TABLESPOON FRESH LEMON JUICE

1 CUP GRANULATED SUGAR, PLUS 2 TABLESPOONS

3 TABLESPOONS ALL-PURPOSE FLOUR

1 STICK OF UNSALTED BUTTER

1 CUP LIGHT BROWN SUGAR

2 FLAKY PASTRY CRUSTS (SEE PAGE 184)

1 EGG WHITE

DIRECTIONS

1 Position a grate over the fire using gloved hands and tongs. Make sure the grate is as secure and level as possible.

2 Put the blueberries in a large bowl and add the lemon juice, 1 cup of granulated sugar, and flour. Stir to combine.

3 When the coals are glowing, melt the butter in a 10-inch cast-iron skillet. Add the brown sugar and cook, while stirring constantly, until the brown sugar is dissolved, 1 or 2 minutes. Remove pan from heat.

4 Gently place one crust over the butter-and-sugar mixture. Fill with the blueberries and place the other crust over the blueberries, crimping the edges together.

5 Brush the top crust with the egg white and then sprinkle the remaining granulated sugar over it. Cut 4 or 5 slits in the middle.

6 Cover and bake for 50 minutes to 1 hour, turning every few minutes to avoid burn spots, until the pie is golden brown and bubbly.

7 Allow to cool before serving.

TIP: If you feel like adding a decorative touch to your pie, cut your second crust into strips and lay them across the top to make a picture-perfect lattice crust.

Cherry Pie

YIELD: 4 TO 6 SERVINGS • ACTIVE TIME: 30 MINUTES • TOTAL TIME: 1 HOUR AND 30 MINUTES

Nothing heralds the true start of spring like cherry blossoms, and what better way to showcase that beautiful display than using the resulting fruits to make an irresistible pie?

INGREDIENTS

4 CUPS CHERRIES (DARK OR RAINIER PREFERRED), PITTED

2 CUPS SUGAR

2 TABLESPOONS FRESH LEMON JUICE

3 TABLESPOONS CORNSTARCH

1 TABLESPOON WATER

¼ TEASPOON ALMOND EXTRACT

2 FLAKY PASTRY CRUSTS (SEE PAGE 184)

1 EGG, BEATEN

DIRECTIONS

1 Position a grate over the fire using gloved hands and tongs. Make sure the grate is as secure and level as possible. When the coals are glowing, place the cherries, sugar, and lemon juice in a saucepan and cook, while stirring occasionally, until the mixture is syrupy.

2 Combine the cornstarch and water in a small bowl and stir this mixture into the saucepan. Move the pan to the edge of the fire and cook, while stirring, until the mixture is thick. Remove from heat, add the almond extract, and let cool.

3 When the cherry mixture has cooled, place the bottom crust in a greased 10-inch cast-iron skillet and pour the cherry mixture into the crust. Top with the other crust, make a few slits in the top, and brush the top crust with the beaten egg.

4 Cover and bake, turning every few minutes to avoid burn spots, until the top crust is golden brown, about 45 minutes. Remove and let cool before serving.

Pecan Pie

YIELD: 8 TO 10 SERVINGS • ACTIVE TIME: 30 MINUTES • TOTAL TIME: 1 HOUR AND 30 MINUTES

This simple dessert of nuts, eggs, sugar, and vanilla is associated with the South, especially Louisiana. Credit for its creation, however, is partly owed to the French, who used the newly discovered nut in a dessert during their early days in the territory.

INGREDIENTS

3 EGGS

1 CUP DARK CORN SYRUP

½ CUP SUGAR

4 TABLESPOONS UNSALTED BUTTER, MELTED

1 TEASPOON VANILLA EXTRACT

1 CUP PECAN HALVES OR BROKEN PIECES

1 FLAKY PASTRY CRUST (SEE PAGE 184)

DIRECTIONS

1 Position a grate over the fire using gloved hands and tongs. Make sure the grate is as secure and level as possible.

2 In a large bowl, whisk the eggs until thoroughly combined. Add the corn syrup, sugar, melted butter, and vanilla. Whisk until combined, then stir in the pecan pieces.

3 Working with the crust in a 10-inch cast-iron skillet, transfer the filling into the pie crust, shaking the skillet gently so that the filling is distributed evenly.

4 When the coals are glowing, cover the skillet and bake, turning every few minutes to avoid burn spots, for about 1 hour, or until a knife inserted in the center comes out clean.

5 Allow to cool to room temperature before serving.

TIP: If you intend to remove the pie before serving, make sure you grease the skillet with butter or cooking spray before cooking. When the pie is cooked and completely cooled, it will be possible to slide the pie out with the help of a thin plastic spatula. However, greasing the skillet in this manner will lend the bottom crust a slightly rough texture.

Chocolate & Bourbon Pecan Pie

YIELD: 8 TO 10 SERVINGS • ACTIVE TIME: 45 MINUTES • TOTAL TIME: 2 HOURS

Here's another step up in the pecan pie department. If you're looking to make a pie that will have your friends and family raving about your cooking, this is the one!

INGREDIENTS

1½ CUPS PECANS

1 FLAKY PASTRY CRUST
(SEE PAGE 184)

6 OZ. SEMISWEET CHOCOLATE
CHIPS

1 CUP DARK CORN SYRUP

⅓ CUP GRANULATED SUGAR

½ CUP FIRMLY PACKED LIGHT
BROWN SUGAR

¼ CUP BOURBON

4 LARGE EGGS

4 TABLESPOONS UNSALTED
BUTTER, MELTED

2 TEASPOONS VANILLA EXTRACT

½ TEASPOON TABLE SALT

DIRECTIONS

1 Position a grate over the fire using gloved hands and tongs. Make sure the grate is as secure and level as possible.

2 When the coals are glowing, spread the pecan pieces on the bottom of a 12-inch cast-iron skillet. Bake for 6 to 10 minutes, checking often to make sure they don't burn. When fragrant, remove from the fire and let cool. Chop pecans into small pieces and set aside.

3 Move the skillet further from the center of the fire.

4 Working with the crust in the skillet, sprinkle the toasted pecan pieces and chocolate chips evenly onto the crust.

5 In a saucepan, combine the corn syrup, granulated sugar, light brown sugar, and bourbon. Stir to combine and cook, while stirring constantly, until the mixture just comes to a boil. Remove from heat.

6 In a large bowl, whisk the eggs until thoroughly combined. Add the melted butter, vanilla, and salt, and whisk to combine. Add about ¼ of the sugar-and-bourbon mixture to the egg mixture, whisking briskly to combine so the eggs don't curdle or cook. When thoroughly combined, continue to add the hot liquid to the egg mixture in small amounts, whisking to combine thoroughly after each addition until all of it is incorporated. Pour this mixture over the nuts and chocolate pieces and shake the skillet gently to distribute evenly.

Continued...

7 Cover the skillet and bake for 1 hour, turning every few minutes to avoid burn spots. Bake until a knife inserted toward the middle comes out clean. Allow to cool completely before serving.

Pumpkin Pie

YIELD: 6 TO 8 SERVINGS • ACTIVE TIME: 30 MINUTES • TOTAL TIME: 1 HOUR AND 30 MINUTES

With the butter-and-sugar combo underneath the pie shell, the result is a crisp, sweet crust topped with an earthy, smooth pumpkin filling. It really works.

INGREDIENTS

1 (14 OZ.) CAN PUMPKIN PUREE
(NOT PUMPKIN PIE FILLING)

1 (12 OZ.) CAN EVAPORATED MILK

2 EGGS, LIGHTLY BEATEN

½ CUP SUGAR

½ TEASPOON SALT

1 TEASPOON CINNAMON

¼ TEASPOON GROUND GINGER

¼ TEASPOON GROUND NUTMEG

1 TABLESPOON UNSALTED BUTTER

1 TABLESPOON LIGHT BROWN
SUGAR

1 FLAKY PASTRY CRUST
(SEE PAGE 184)

DIRECTIONS

1 Position a grate over the fire using gloved hands and tongs. Make sure the grate is as secure and level as possible.

2 In a large bowl, combine the pumpkin puree, evaporated milk, eggs, sugar, salt, cinnamon, ginger, and nutmeg. Stir to combine thoroughly.

3 When the coals are glowing, melt the butter in a 12-inch cast-iron skillet. Add the brown sugar and cook, while stirring constantly, for 1 to 2 minutes, until the sugar is dissolved. Carefully remove the skillet from heat.

4 Place the pie crust over the sugar mixture. Fill with the pumpkin mixture.

5 Cover the skillet and bake for 15 minutes, turning the skillet every few minutes to avoid burn spots, then move the skillet further from the center of the fire and bake for an additional 30 to 45 minutes, or until the filling is firm and a toothpick inserted in the middle comes out clean. Don't overcook.

6 Remove the skillet from heat and allow to cool before serving. Serve with whipped cream.

Double Lemon Tart

YIELD: 6 TO 8 SERVINGS • ACTIVE TIME: 30 MINUTES • TOTAL TIME: 1 HOUR

Lemons are like sunshine—they brighten everything! Very thinly sliced lemons sit atop a lemon-drenched custard to make a dessert whose flavor shines from the first bite to the last.

INGREDIENTS

1 (14 OZ.) CAN OF SWEETENED CONDENSED MILK

½ CUP FRESH LEMON JUICE

4 LARGE EGG YOLKS

1 TABLESPOON VANILLA EXTRACT

1 GRAHAM CRACKER CRUST (SEE PAGE 187)

1 LEMON, SEEDED AND SLICED VERY THIN

DIRECTIONS

1 Position a grate over the fire using gloved hands and tongs. Make sure the grate is as secure and level as possible.

2 In a medium bowl, combine the condensed milk, lemon juice, egg yolks, and vanilla. Working with the crust in a 10-inch cast-iron skillet, pour the filling into the crust. Top with the very thin slices of lemon, arranged in a decorative pattern.

3 When the coals are glowing, cover and bake, turning the skillet every few minutes to avoid burn spots, for about 15 to 20 minutes, until the liquid has set into a soft custard. If not done, check every 5 minutes until done to your liking.

4 Allow to cool completely before serving.

French Apple Tart

YIELD: 6 TO 8 SERVINGS • ACTIVE TIME: 1 HOUR • TOTAL TIME: 2 TO 24 HOURS

Cast-iron skillets caramelize fruits to perfection. This recipe is the quintessential example. It's what the French call "tarte Tatin," and for them it's a national treasure.

INGREDIENTS

1 CUP ALL-PURPOSE FLOUR, PLUS MORE FOR DUSTING

½ TEASPOON SALT

1½ CUPS SUGAR, PLUS 1 TABLESPOON

2 STICKS OF UNSALTED BUTTER, CUT INTO SMALL PIECES

3 TABLESPOONS ICE WATER

8 APPLES, PEELED, CORED, AND SLICED

DIRECTIONS

1 To make the pastry, whisk together the flour, salt, and 1 tablespoon of sugar in a large bowl. Using your fingers, work 6 tablespoons of the butter into the flour mixture until you have coarse clumps. Sprinkle the ice water over the mixture and continue to work it with your hands until the dough just holds together. Shape it into a ball, wrap it in plastic wrap, and chill it for at least 1 hour or overnight.

2 Position a grate over the fire using gloved hands and tongs. Make sure the grate is as secure and level as possible. When the coals are glowing, place the remaining pieces of butter evenly over the bottom of a 12-inch cast-iron skillet, then sprinkle the remaining sugar evenly over everything. Next, start placing the apple slices in a circular pattern, starting at the edge of the skillet and working in. The slices should overlap and face the same direction. Place either 1 or 2 slices in the center when finished working around the outside. As the tart bakes, the slices will slide down a bit.

3 When the coals are glowing, place the skillet over the center of the fire. Cook, turning the skillet every few minutes to avoid burn spots, until the juices in the pan are a deep amber color, about 10 minutes. Remove from heat and turn the apples over. Place the skillet back over the fire, cook for another 5 minutes, and then remove from heat.

4 Take the chilled dough out of the cooler and, working on a lightly floured surface, roll it out into a circle (about 12 to 14 inches). Taking care not to burn your fingers on the hot skillet, drape the pastry over the apples and pinch it in around the sides.

Continued...

5 Cover and bake, turning the skillet every few minutes to avoid burn spots, for about 25 minutes, or until the pastry is golden brown.

6 Allow to cool for about 5 minutes. Find a plate that is an inch or 2 larger than the top of the skillet and place it over the top. You will be inverting the tart onto the plate. Be sure to use oven mitts or secure pot holders, as the skillet will be hot.

7 Holding the plate tightly against the top, turn the skillet over so the plate is now on the bottom. If some of the apples are stuck to the bottom, gently remove them and place them on the tart. Allow to cool a few more minutes, or set aside until ready to serve. The tart is best served warm.

Dutch Apple Baby

YIELD: 4 SERVINGS • ACTIVE TIME: 45 MINUTES • TOTAL TIME: 1 HOUR AND 15 MINUTES

This is a classic cast iron recipe for a pastry that puffs up in the skillet. It is reminiscent of the recipe for David Eyre's Pancake (see page 22).

INGREDIENTS

2 FIRM, SEMI-TART APPLES (MUTSU OR GOLDEN DELICIOUS), PEELED AND CORED

4 TABLESPOONS UNSALTED BUTTER

¼ CUP SUGAR, PLUS 3 TABLESPOONS

1 TABLESPOON CINNAMON

¾ CUP ALL-PURPOSE FLOUR

¼ TEASPOON SALT

¾ CUP WHOLE MILK

4 EGGS

1 TEASPOON VANILLA OR ALMOND EXTRACT

CONFECTIONERS' SUGAR, FOR DUSTING

DIRECTIONS

1 Position a grate over the fire using gloved hands and tongs. Make sure the grate is as secure and level as possible.

2 Cut the apples into slices. When the coals are glowing, heat a 10-inch cast-iron skillet over the fire. Add the butter and apples and cook, while stirring, for 3 to 4 minutes, until the apples soften. Add the ¼ cup of sugar and cinnamon and continue cooking for another 3 or 4 minutes. Distribute the apples evenly over the bottom of the skillet and remove from heat.

3 In a large bowl, mix the remaining sugar, flour, and salt together. In a smaller bowl, whisk together the milk, eggs, and vanilla or almond extract. Add the wet ingredients to the dry ingredients and stir to combine. Pour the batter over the apples.

4 Cover and bake, turning the skillet every few minutes to avoid burn spots, for 15 to 20 minutes, until the "baby" is puffy and browned on the top.

5 Allow to cool for a few minutes. Run a knife along the edge of the skillet to loosen the dessert. Put a plate over the skillet and, using oven mitts or pot holders, flip it over so the dessert is transferred to the plate. Serve warm with a dusting of confectioners' sugar.

Peach Galette

YIELD: 6 TO 8 SERVINGS • ACTIVE TIME: 45 MINUTES • TOTAL TIME: 1 HOUR AND 30 MINUTES

When peaches are ripe in the mid-to-late summer, this is a super-simple way to turn them into a great dessert. Smearing some peach jam on the crust before adding the fruit will intensify the flavor, and if you want something a little more "adult," consider adding some Amaretto or bourbon to the jam.

INGREDIENTS

1 FLAKY PASTRY CRUST
(SEE PAGE 184)

3 CUPS FRESH PEACHES, PEELED
(OPTIONAL), PITTED, AND SLICED

½ CUP SUGAR, PLUS 1 TABLESPOON

JUICE OF ½ LEMON

3 TABLESPOONS CORNSTARCH

PINCH OF SALT

1 TEASPOON AMARETTO OR
BOURBON (OPTIONAL)

2 TABLESPOONS PEACH JAM

1 EGG, BEATEN

DIRECTIONS

1 Position a grate over the fire using gloved hands and tongs. Make sure the grate is as secure and level as possible.

2 Place the crust in a greased 10-inch cast-iron skillet.

3 In a large bowl, mix the peaches with the ½ cup of sugar, lemon juice, cornstarch, and salt. Stir well to coat all the fruit.

4 If using the Amaretto or bourbon, mix it with the jam in a small bowl before brushing or smearing the jam over the center of the crust.

5 Place the peaches in a mound in the center of the crust. Fold the edge of the crust over to cover about 1 inch of filling. Brush the crust with the beaten egg and sprinkle it with the remaining sugar.

6 When the coals are glowing, cover and bake until the filling is bubbly, which is necessary for it to thicken, about 35 to 40 minutes, turning the skillet every few minutes to avoid burn spots. If not done, check every 5 minutes until cooked to your liking.

7 Let cool before serving.

Plum Galette

YIELD: 4 TO 6 SERVINGS • ACTIVE TIME: 40 MINUTES • TOTAL TIME: 1 HOUR AND 30 MINUTES

Here's another summer fruit–laden treat that is so easy to put together and tastes great! The flavor of the plums is definitely enhanced by the jam, and the whole thing is sublime when topped with ice cream and roasted and salted pumpkin seeds.

INGREDIENTS

1 FLAKY PASTRY CRUST
(SEE PAGE 184)

3 CUPS FRESH PLUMS, PITTED
AND SLICED

½ CUP SUGAR, PLUS 1 TABLESPOON

JUICE OF ½ LEMON

3 TABLESPOONS CORNSTARCH

PINCH OF SALT

2 TABLESPOONS BLACKBERRY JAM

1 EGG, BEATEN

DIRECTIONS

1 Position a grate over the fire using gloved hands and tongs. Make sure the grate is as secure and level as possible.

2 Place the crust in a greased 10-inch cast-iron skillet.

3 In a large bowl, mix the plums with ½ cup of the sugar, lemon juice, cornstarch, and salt. Stir well to coat all the fruit.

4 Brush or smear the jam over the center of the crust. Place the plums in a mound in the center. Fold the edges of the crust over to cover about 1 inch of the filling. Brush the crust with the beaten egg and sprinkle it with the remaining sugar.

5 When the coals are glowing, cover and bake until the filling is bubbly, which is necessary for it to thicken, about 35 to 40 minutes, turning the skillet every few minutes to avoid burn spots. If not done, check every 5 minutes until cooked to your liking.

6 Let cool before serving.

The Best Skillet Brownies

YIELD: 6 TO 8 SERVINGS • ACTIVE TIME: 40 MINUTES • TOTAL TIME: 1 HOUR AND 30 MINUTES

If you're serious about brownies, you'll love this recipe. When shopping for the ingredients, remember that the better the chocolate, the better the taste and texture of the brownie. What gets baked up in the cast-iron skillet is a gooey yet crunchy confection that is heaven in every bite. Don't even slice them up—serve them right out of the skillet (when cool enough). Just be sure to have friends and family around when you do, as you may be tempted to eat the whole pan by yourself.

INGREDIENTS

10 TABLESPOONS UNSALTED BUTTER

½ LB. SEMISWEET CHOCOLATE, COARSELY CHOPPED

1 CUP SUGAR

3 EGGS, AT ROOM TEMPERATURE

1 TEASPOON VANILLA EXTRACT

½ CUP ALL-PURPOSE FLOUR, PLUS 2 TABLESPOONS

2 TABLESPOONS UNSWEETENED COCOA POWDER

¼ TEASPOON SALT

1 CUP SEMISWEET CHOCOLATE CHIPS

DIRECTIONS

1 Position a grate over the fire using gloved hands and tongs. Make sure the grate is as secure and level as possible.

2 When the coals are glowing, melt 9 tablespoons of the butter and chopped chocolate pieces together in a heat-proof bowl, cooking in 15-second increments and stirring after each, until the butter and chocolate are just melted together and smooth.

3 In a large bowl, add the sugar and eggs and whisk to combine. Add the vanilla and stir to combine. Working in batches, start mixing the melted chocolate into the mixture, stirring vigorously to combine after each addition. In a small bowl, mix the flour, cocoa powder, and salt. Gently fold the dry mixture into the chocolate mixture. Next, fold in the chocolate chips.

4 Melt the remaining butter in a 12-inch cast-iron skillet. When melted, pour in the batter. Cover and bake, turning the skillet every few minutes to avoid burn spots, for about 30 minutes, or until a toothpick inserted in the center comes out with a few moist crumbs. It may need a couple more minutes, but be careful not to overbake this or you'll lose the gooeyness that makes these brownies so great. When the brownies are ready, remove from heat and allow to cool for about 10 minutes.

5 Dig right in, or scoop into bowls and serve.

VARIATION: To give the brownies a refreshing zing, add 1½ teaspoon of peppermint extract and 1 cups of chopped York Peppermint Patties to the batter.

Classic Shortbread Wedges

YIELD: 6 TO 8 SERVINGS • ACTIVE TIME: 25 MINUTES • TOTAL TIME: 1 HOUR

Shortbread is wonderfully simple to prepare and so, so yummy. The butter shines through in each flaky bite. These wedges are the perfect late-afternoon pick-me-up when served with coffee, tea, or hot chocolate.

INGREDIENTS

1 CUP ALL-PURPOSE FLOUR, PLUS MORE FOR DUSTING

¼ TEASPOON SALT

¼ CUP SUGAR

1 STICK OF UNSALTED BUTTER, CHILLED

½ TEASPOON VANILLA EXTRACT

DIRECTIONS

1 Position a grate over the fire using gloved hands and tongs. Make sure the grate is as secure and level as possible. Warm a 12-inch cast-iron skillet while making the dough.

2 In a large bowl, combine the flour, salt, and sugar, whisking to combine.

3 Cut the butter into slices and add to the flour mixture. The best way to work it into the flour is with your hands. As it starts to come together, add the vanilla extract. Work the mixture until it resembles coarse meal.

4 Gather the dough into a ball. On a lightly floured surface, roll it out into a circle. Slice the round into 8 wedges.

5 When the coals are glowing, place the wedges in the skillet to recreate the circle of dough. Cover and bake, turning the skillet every few minutes to avoid burn spots, for about 45 minutes or until the shortbread is a pale golden color. Allow to cool for about 10 minutes before transferring the cookies to a plate.

Strawberry Rhubarb Crisp

YIELD: 4 SERVINGS • ACTIVE TIME: 30 MINUTES • TOTAL TIME: 1 HOUR

This magnificent combo traditionally appears in a pie, but this crisp allows you to enjoy it without all of the fuss.

INGREDIENTS

1½ CUPS CHOPPED RHUBARB

1½ CUPS HULLED AND SLICED STRAWBERRIES

2 TABLESPOONS GRANULATED SUGAR

⅓ CUP ALL-PURPOSE FLOUR, PLUS 2 TEASPOONS

4 TABLESPOONS UNSALTED BUTTER, CHILLED AND CUT INTO PIECES

¼ CUP DARK BROWN SUGAR

¾ CUP QUICK-COOKING OATS

¼ CUP CHOPPED HAZELNUTS (OPTIONAL)

WHIPPED CREAM, FOR SERVING (OPTIONAL)

ICE CREAM, FOR SERVING (OPTIONAL)

DIRECTIONS

1 Position a grate over the fire using gloved hands and tongs. Make sure the grate is as secure and level as possible.

2 In a bowl, combine the rhubarb pieces, strawberries, granulated sugar, and the 2 teaspoons of flour, and toss to coat the fruit. Transfer to a 10-inch cast-iron skillet.

3 In another bowl, add the butter and brown sugar and work the mixture with a fork or pastry blender. Add the oats, hazelnuts (if using), and remaining flour and continue to work the mixture until it is a coarse meal. Sprinkle it over the fruit in the skillet.

4 When the coals are glowing, cover the skillet and bake, turning the skillet every few minutes to avoid burn spots, for about 30 minutes, until the topping is golden and the fruit is bubbly. Serve warm with whipped cream or ice cream.

Apple & Pear Crumble

YIELD: 4 TO 6 SERVINGS • ACTIVE TIME: 30 MINUTES • TOTAL TIME: 45 MINUTES

The tart pop of the Cortland apples and the sweet softness of the red pears give this dish a wonderful balance, and adding freshly grated ginger to the topping really sets it apart.

INGREDIENTS

FOR THE TOPPING

½ CUP WHOLE WHEAT FLOUR

1 STICK OF UNSALTED BUTTER, CUT INTO SMALL PIECES

½ CUP OATS

½ CUP BROWN SUGAR

¼ CUP GRANULATED SUGAR

1 TABLESPOON GRATED GINGER

½ TEASPOON CINNAMON

½ TEASPOON NUTMEG

½ TEASPOON KOSHER SALT

FOR THE FILLING

2 TABLESPOONS UNSALTED BUTTER

PINCH OF KOSHER SALT

2 TABLESPOONS BROWN SUGAR

2 TABLESPOONS TAPIOCA STARCH OR CORNSTARCH

3 CORTLAND APPLES, EACH PEELED, QUARTERED, AND CUT INTO 20 EVEN SLICES

3 RED PEARS, EACH PEELED, QUARTERED, AND CUT INTO 16 EVEN SLICES

Continued...

DIRECTIONS

1 Position a grate over the fire using gloved hands and tongs. Make sure the grate is as secure and level as possible.

2 To prepare the topping, place all of the ingredients in a large mixing bowl and use a fork to mash the butter and other ingredients together. Continue until the topping is a collection of pea-sized pieces. Place the bowl in the cooler.

3 When the coals are glowing, add the butter to a 8-inch cast-iron skillet. Place the salt, brown sugar, and tapioca starch or cornstarch in a bowl and stir to combine.

4 Once the butter has melted, put the apple slices in the pan in one even layer, working from the outside toward the center. Cook for 5 to 7 minutes.

5 Sprinkle half of the brown sugar mixture over the apples.

6 Utilizing the same technique you used for the apple slices, layer all of the pear slices in the skillet. Sprinkle the remaining brown sugar mixture on top. Top with any remaining apple slices.

7 Combine the vanilla extract, almond extract, and lemon juice in a bowl and pour over all of the fruit.

8 Remove the topping from the cooler and spread in an even layer on top of the fruit. Cover the skillet and bake for 15 minutes, turning the skillet every few minutes to avoid burn spots.

9 Remove the cover and bake for another 20 minutes.

Continued...

1 TABLESPOON VANILLA EXTRACT

1 TABLESPOON ALMOND EXTRACT

JUICE OF ½ LEMON

ICE CREAM, FOR SERVING
(OPTIONAL)

WHIPPED CREAM, FOR SERVING
(OPTIONAL)

10 If you would like the crisp to set, let the skillet rest on the edge of the fire for another 20 minutes. Or remove the skillet from heat, top the crisp with your favorite ice cream or whipped cream, and serve.

METRIC CONVERSIONS

U.S. Measurement	Approximate Metric Liquid Measurement	Approximate Metric Dry Measurement
1 teaspoon	5 ml	5 g
1 tablespoon or ½ ounce	15 ml	14 g
1 ounce or ⅛ cup	30 ml	29 g
¼ cup or 2 ounces	60 ml	57 g
⅓ cup	80 ml	76 g
½ cup or 4 ounces	120 ml	113 g
⅔ cup	160 ml	151 g
¾ cup or 6 ounces	180 ml	170 g
1 cup or 8 ounces or ½ pint	240 ml	227 g
1½ cups or 12 ounces	350 ml	340 g
2 cups or 1 pint or 16 ounces	475 ml	454 g
3 cups or 1½ pints	700 ml	680 g
4 cups or 2 pints or 1 quart	950 ml	908 g

INDEX

INDEX

INDEX

INDEX

About Cider Mill Press Book Publishers

Good ideas ripen with time. From seed to harvest, Cider Mill Press brings fine reading, information, and entertainment together between the covers of its creatively crafted books. Our Cider Mill bears fruit twice a year, publishing a new crop of titles each spring and fall.

CIDER MILL PRESS

BOOK PUBLISHERS

"Where Good Books Are Ready for Press"

Visit us online at
cidermillpress.com

or write to us at
PO Box 454
12 Spring St.
Kennebunkport, Maine 04046